Black September

Black September

Its Short, Violent History

CHRISTOPHER DOBSON

MACMILLAN PUBLISHING CO., INC.

NEW YORK

COLLIER MACMILLAN PUBLISHERS

LONDON

Macmillan Publishing Co., Inc.
866 Third Avenue, New York, N.Y. 10022
Collier-Macmillan Canada Ltd.

Library of Congress Cataloging in Publication Data

Dobson, Christopher.
    Black September.

    1. Munaẓẓamat Aylūl al-Aswad.   2. Fedayeen.
3. Jewish-Arab relations—1967–1973.   I. Title.
DS119.7.D615 1974   320.9'569   74-11121
ISBN 0-02-531900-0

First Printing 1974

Printed in the United States of America

ACKNOWLEDGMENTS

I WISH TO thank my colleagues of the *Daily* and *Sunday Telegraph* for their help in the collection and interpretation of material from all over the world. As usual, they did a first-class job of professional journalism. I would also like to thank my Arab and Jewish friends who helped me with interviews, advice and, eventually, protection.

To my wife, Shirley

Contents

FOREWORD   ix

1   *The Deadly Birth*   1

2   *The Holy Cause*   42

3   *The Fatal Flaw*   56

4   *The Killing at Lod*   65

5   *The Massacre at Munich*   80

6   *The Wrath of God*   89

7   *Kill and Counterkill*   110

8   *The Danger in Europe*   134

9   *Death and Dissension*   150

10   *The Day of Atonement*   162

INDEX   173

Foreword

THIS BOOK HAS been developed from a series of long articles written for the *Sunday Telegraph* of London. My Arab friends were furious with me for exposing many of the secrets of Black September. I was called a traitor to their cause and my life was threatened. Inevitably this work will be judged in the same way, and in the blindly emotional world of Middle Eastern politics it will be taken as an attack on the Palestinians' struggle for the redress of quite genuine grievances. This is quite wrong. What I have done is to try to tell the true story of Arab terrorism today and to show how cruel and, in the end, counterproductive it is. I abhor terrorism of all sorts, Israeli or Arab or World Revolutionary. There can never be any excuse for the taking of innocent lives in the ruthless fashion of the massacres at Lod and Rome airports. And there can be no excuse for the way in which the Israelis shot down an unarmed

Libyan airliner over the Sinai. There now seems, after the War of the Day of Atonement, that there is a small glimmer of light in the bloody gloom of Arab-Israeli relations. Inevitably terrorism will continue. It has become a way of life—and death —for too many people for it to be abandoned. But if this book helps in any way to curb the killing, then I shall be very happy.

Black September

1 • The Deadly Birth

BLACK SEPTEMBER was born in violence with a flurry of pistol shots in the quietly lush foyer of Cairo's Sheraton Hotel in the early afternoon of November 28, 1971. Five of those shots, fired at point-blank range, hit Wasfi Tell, the fifty-two-year-old Prime Minister of Jordan. He staggered back against the shattered swing doors, trying to draw his own gun, but his strength had already left him and he fell dying among the shards of glass on the marble floor. As he lay there one of his killers bent over and lapped the blood that poured from his wounds. It was an act which symbolized Black September's absolute rejection of normal standards of behavior.

There were six in the assassination squad; the organizer who provided arms and money and set up the killing, the four young men who carried it out, and a girl, a student in Cairo, whose task was to throw a grenade at Tell if the young men missed.

But they did not fail, and while they were being arrested after a wild chase through the hotel, she slipped away and went back to her studies.

Once they were caught the killers not only confessed willingly, they rejoiced in their triumph. Monzer Khalifa, the blood drinker, lifted his hand in a victory sign and told the police: "I am proud. Finally I have done it. We have been after him for six months. We have taken our revenge on a traitor." Essat Rabah, the man who fired the fatal shots, said: "We wanted to have him for breakfast but we had him for lunch instead."

Khalifa then told the police how he and Rabah had been walking together in Beirut fifteen days before when they heard that Tell was going to Cairo to lead his country's delegation to the Arab Defense Council: "We jumped for joy and embraced for this was the chance of a lifetime to destroy him." They flew to Cairo, were installed in an apartment and given pistols and grenades. On the day of the killing they took up their positions in the foyer of the hotel with their two companions, Ziad Helou and Jawal Khalil Baghdady, just after Tell had left for the Arab League Headquarters on the other side of the Nile.

While they waited for him to return, they ate sandwiches, drank Coca-Cola and watched the American tourists passing through on their way to see the Pyramids. Nobody paid any attention to the terrorists even though the hotel is only three blocks away from President Sadat's heavily guarded villa on the west bank of the Nile. Cairo still is one of the crossroads of the world and its hotels are filled with people of many kinds and colors. On this particular day Wasfi Tell's wife was herself having lunch in the crowded cafeteria on the ground floor where the killers bought their Coca-Cola. The four young Palestinians were accepted as a natural part of this cosmopolitan scene.

Tell himself was aware of the dangers he ran. He knew he

had been sentenced to death by the Palestinian commandos for the part he played in destroying their power in Jordan in September 1970. A veteran of Middle Eastern politics, in which differences of policy are often settled with a bullet or a dagger, he always carried a gun and was surrounded by bodyguards. But as he walked up the steps of the hotel, returning the salute of the blue-uniformed doorman, his guard was down. He had just been to a lunch given for him and his colleagues by Abdul Khalek Hassouna, Secretary-General of the Arab League, there was no indication of trouble, he was well protected and the American-womb haven of the hotel lay through the swinging doors. He stood no chance. "I saw him coming from his car," Rabah told the police, "and when he opened the door I fired the five bullets in my pistol into him." Mrs. Tell heard those shots and ran into the foyer to find her husband lying dead. Arab women do not mourn quietly. "Are you happy Arabs?" she screamed. "What a loss you have caused. Palestine is finished." And she cursed the killer with the worst of Moslem insults: "Arabs are sons of bitches!" King Hussein, weeping at his friend's state funeral in the Royal Cemetery in Amman the following day, was just as bitter: "The tragedy is not death, but the degree to which cowards and subhumans will stoop."

Hussein is no stranger to assassination. When he was sixteen, his grandfather, King Abdullah, was shot down alongside him on the steps of the El Aqsa mosque in Jerusalem, and he has lost count of the number of attempts made on his own life. But what he did not know was that the killing of Wasfi Tell was to mark a major turning point in the evolution of violence, not only in the Middle East but throughout the world, for the success of the killing prompted the revelation in a jubilant announcement from Beirut that it had been carried out by a new and secret group which was dedicated to revenge and which had taken its name from the disastrous month when Hussein and his loyal Bedouin soldiers had smashed the Palestinian guerrillas. It was Black September.

3

Secret societies which use murder and terror as instruments of policy run like a scarlet thread through Arab history. The Moslem Brotherhood, which was founded by Hassan el Banna in Ismailia in 1928 as a society of religious resurgence based on the Koran, became so powerful that in the early 1950s it claimed a membership of two million spread throughout the Arab world, and while most of them were peaceful religious people dedicated to Islam, its leaders were fanatics who used their spiritual power in a struggle for temporal power which made them a force to be reckoned with in every Moslem country. And what they could not achieve by prayer and political maneuvering they achieved through a terrorist branch, known as the Secret Organ, that was feared throughout the Middle East. Its main weapon was the assassination of political leaders who refused to carry out the Brotherhood's orders. President Sadat of Egypt, where the Brotherhood was strongest, had close associations with this terrorist branch and was implicated in several of its operations. President Nasser also dickered with joining the Brotherhood and maintained contact with it when he was plotting the overthrow of King Farouk. But Nasser had no taste for terrorism and when, as a lieutenant colonel, he took part in an attempt to kill General Hussein Sirry Amer, one of the King's cronies, he failed and was happy to have done so. In his book *Philosophy of the Revolution,* he told the story of the attempt: "The detonation of our arms, immediately followed by the heart-rending cries of a woman and the sound of a frightened child, haunted me all the way to my bed and kept me awake all night. Remorse gripped my heart. . . . I stammered, 'If only he does not die.' By dawn I had arrived at the point where I prayed for the life of the man I had tried to kill—how great was my joy when, feverishly searching the morning newspaper, I discovered that the man had not succumbed."

It was one of those constant paradoxes of the Arab world— an unsuccessful attempt on Nasser's life—which led to the destruction of the Brotherhood's power. In 1954 Nasser signed a treaty with Britain settling the problems of the Canal Zone. The Brotherhood objected violently to this agreement claiming that it was another colonial treaty with Britain and was therefore a betrayal of the people. And they determined to kill Nasser. The attempt took place as he was addressing an open-air meeting in Alexandria on October 26, 1954. The would-be killer, a simple-minded tinsmith called Mahmoud Abdul Latif, emptied his revolver at Nasser but managed to hit only the light bulb swinging over Nasser's head. He struck back, arrested thousands of the Brothers, sending their leader, Hassan el Hodeiby, to prison for life and hanging not only the tinsmith and three others directly concerned in the plot but also two members of the Brotherhood's Supreme Guidance Council, Abdul el Kader Auda and Sheikh Mohammed Farghaly. The Brotherhood was crushed. And the man the fanatics set out to kill behaved so bravely under fire that his popularity, which had been languishing, was restored overnight and enabled him to get rid of the figurehead General Neguib and finally emerge as President of Egypt.

Another secret organization dedicated to terror was founded by Haj Amin el Husseini, the Mufti of Jerusalem, who is bitterly anti-Zionist and has devoted his life to trying to prevent the establishment of a Jewish state in Palestine. His followers would kill anybody, Arab or Jew, they suspected of opposing his policies. It was he who was responsible for the anti-Jewish riots in Jerusalem in 1920, and in 1936 he launched an armed uprising against the Jewish settlers which cost two thousand lives. He, above all others, was responsible for the fear that grew between the two communities in Palestine. During World War II he threw in his lot with Hitler but escaped from Germany after the war to return to the Middle East to carry on his murderous policies. He was heavily implicated in the assassination of King Abdullah of Jordan when it was thought the King might make peace with Israel, and it was he who urged his followers to kill in a Jihad, a Holy War, against the Jews in 1947, a war which was to end in disaster for the Arabs of Palestine and disgrace for Haj Amin, who now lives in Beirut, still yearning for power, still hating the Jews.

But, while the Mufti is deposed and disgraced, and the Moslem Brotherhood broken, their most extreme supporters maintain a strong influence on the modern terrorist organizations. The links are both physical and philosophical. Yasir Arafat, leader of Al Fatah, parent organization of Black September, not only was a member of the Moslem Brotherhood but also belongs to the Mufti's large and powerful clan, his father having been a cousin by marriage of the Mufti. Arafat served as an aide to Abdel Kader el Husseini, the Mufti's nephew and leader of the Arab forces in the war of 1948 until he was killed at the battle of Castel. Another member of the clan, Ghazi Abdel Kader el Husseini, is one of the leaders of both Fatah and Black September. Yet another, Ziad el Husseini, leader of a guerrilla group in Gaza, committed suicide in the house of the Mayor of Gaza as he was about to be arrested by Israeli security forces. Ali Hassan Salameh, one of the fiercest of Black September's chieftains, is married to an el Husseini. What this means is that the campaign of terrorism initiated by the killing of Wasfi Tell is not an isolated example of people being driven to acts of terrorism by despair but is part of a continuing tradition of the use of fear and murder for political ends.

This tradition can be traced back to another secret society with which Black September bears close comparison, a society which was founded nearly nine hundred years ago, lasted for two hundred years and which built its power on the terror inspired by its killers. It was the Society of the Assassins, whose name sprang from its members' addiction to hashish.

They were, in Arabic, "Hashashin" and it is a name which, because of their activities as killers, has come to mean murder for political ends. The Assassins were founded by Hassan ibn Sabah, who, like the Mufti and Hassan el Banna, was a religious teacher. His creed was: "Nothing is true, and all is permitted." His power rested on his "fedawi"—devoted ones— young men who killed at his command. They worked in teams of three and their weapons were long daggers tipped with poison. One of the team would attack the chosen victim and if he failed the others would renew the attempt. Nothing stopped them, certainly not the fear of death, for at his mountain head- quarters of Alamut—the Eagle's Nest—Hassan, who came to be known as the Old Man of the Mountain, had built a secret pleasure garden where tinkling fountains ran with wine; soft music and the scent of flowers filled the air and the loveliest of girls waited for the fedawi. The young men who had been chosen to kill for their master were first drugged in the grim Eagle's Nest, where no signs showed of the garden of delights. Then they were carried to the garden to waken to its joys. Everything was theirs, in days and nights spent in a half-drugged state and devoted to their pleasure. After several days of com- plete sensuality they would be drugged again and carried back to the castle, where they would be told that they had just ex- perienced the delights that awaited them in Paradise. There can be no surprise therefore that they went off on their bloody mis- sions prepared for, even welcoming, death. Their prowess at killing and their fanatic dedication struck fear throughout Arabia. And Hassan, the Old Man of the Mountain, grew powerful on this fear. Rulers who had awakened to find an Assassin's dagger stuck into their pillows were happy to pay tribute to him.

Harold Lamb in his *The Flame of Islam* tells this story: "One influential teacher preached against him, cursing him publicly, and before long an Assassin knelt upon the chest of the too-daring preacher, in the seclusion of his study. A long knife pricked the soft skin of his stomach. After the fedawi had vanished, the preacher no longer cursed the heretics, and his disciples asked him why. 'They have arguments,' said the great man, who was not without humor, 'that cannot be re- futed!'" It was the original version of making an offer that couldn't be refused. Hassan ibn Sabah and his men, safe in their mountain fortresses, wielded power in many lands through the use of terror.

No one who undertakes an international flight can doubt the efficacy of modern-day terror. Baggage checks and body searches for guns and bombs have become part of traveling. At least three major airlines are paying tribute to the terrorists to safeguard their airliners from hijacking. Lufthansa paid five million dollars to get one of their airliners back. The oil-rich sheikdoms of Arabia pay their tributes too, even though their downfall is on the terrorists' program. They pay up not only to support the Palestinian cause but also to protect their oil wells and their lives. The Austrian Chancellor, Dr. Bruno Kreisky, was blackmailed into agreeing to shut down Schonau Castle, the staging post of Jews on their way from Russia to Israel, by terrorists who were holding three of the Jewish immigrants as hostages. Kreisky buckled under the threat that if he reneged on the deal "it would not serve Austria's stability and interests or contribute to the safety of its citizens." Kreisky must feel like the teacher of old that the terrorists "have arguments that cannot be refuted."

The young men and women, the fedayeen, who inspire this sort of fear today are just as ready to kill or be killed as were the fedawi. But where the fedawi were drugged with hashish, the modern assassins are drugged with hatred, and where the fedawi longed only for the sensual delights of the Paradise they had been shown, the fedayeen dream of their Paradise lost: Palestine, a land which most of them have never seen. There are others who take their dream of Paradise even further. Certainly the "freeing of Palestine from the imperialist-Zionist yoke" is their first aim, but after that comes the overthrow of the feudal rulers of Arabia and then the heady vision of World Revolution.

But Palestine comes first. Few people in the West can appreciate the depth of feeling of the Arabs over what they regard as a monstrous injustice inflicted on them; and that injustice is the very existence of the state of Israel on Palestinian soil. They have a love for the actual land which is passed on to children who have little hope of ever seeing it. Children born to refugee parents in Beirut, for example, will not say "I am from Beirut" but "I am from Hebron or Nazareth," the places where their parents lived.

This emotional attachment was expressed by the Palestinian author Nasir ad-Din an-Nashashibi in his book *Return Ticket,* written in 1962. He wrote: "Every year I shall say to my little son: We shall return my son and you will be with me; we shall return; we shall return to our land and walk there barefoot. We'll remove our shoes so that we may feel the holiness of the ground beneath us. We'll blend our souls with its air and earth. We'll walk till we come to the orange trees; we'll feel the sand and water; we'll kiss seed and fruit; we'll sleep in the shade of the first tree we meet; we'll pay homage to the first martyr's grave we come across.

"We'll turn here and there to trace our lives. Where are they? Here with this village square, with this mosque's minaret, with the beloved field, the desolate wall, with the remains of a tottering fence and a building whose traces have been erased. Here are our lives. Each grain of sand teaches us about our life. Do you not remember Jaffa with its delightful shore, Haifa and its lofty mountain, Beth Shean and its fields of crops and fruit, Nazareth and the Christians' bells. Acre and the memories of el Jazzar, Ibrahim Pasha, Napoleon and the fortress, the streets of Jerusalem, my dear Jerusalem, Tiberias and its peaceful shore with the golden waves, Majdal and the remnant of my kin in its land?"

It is from emotion such as this, combined with the brutish existence of the refugee camps and the bitter experience of almost constant defeat, that the hatred has grown which leads a young man to drink the blood of his murdered enemy.

In his book Nashashibi goes on to tell what effect his lyrical description of his land will have on his son: "I shall see the hatred in the eyes of my son and your sons. I shall see how they take revenge. If they do not know how to take revenge, I shall teach them. And if they agree to a truce or peace, I shall fight against them as I fight against my enemy and theirs. I want them to be callous, to be ruthless, to take revenge. I want them to wash away the disaster of 1948 with the blood of those who prevent them from entering their land. Their homeland is dear to them, but revenge is dearer. We'll enter their lairs in Tel Aviv. We'll smash Tel Aviv with axes, guns, hands, fingernails and teeth, while singing the songs of Qibiya, Deir Yassin and Nasir ad-Din. We shall sing the hymns of the triumphant avenging return."

Black September grew from hatred such as this. Wasfi Tell died because of it, for he was held responsible for destroying the commandos who believed that one day they would lead the march into Tel Aviv. It also explains the extraordinary sequel to his murder when the trial of his four killers was turned into a trial of Tell and King Hussein. The assassins' lawyers pleaded that they were justified in shooting Tell because they were "pursuing military combat against their enemies" and that Tell and Hussein were traitors and enemies of the Arab people. Ahmed Shukairy, the discredited leader of the Palestine Liberation Organization, who had boasted before the Six Day War of June 1967 that the Jews would be driven into the sea, was brought out of obscurity by the defense to argue that "an end to the present Jordanian regime means an end to all Arab disasters." He described Tell as a tool of imperialism, and said that his elimination was an omen that "similar agents are about to meet the same fate." The Egyptian authorities came under enormous pressure from the rest of the Arab world, particularly President Qaddafi of Libya, to free the assassins. Unlimited funds were allocated for their defense and eventually the Egyptians bowed to the pressure and released them on bail of one thousand Egyptian pounds each. They were never brought back to trial. For a year they lived in comfort in Cairo with spending money provided by Qaddafi. But then they addressed an appeal to Egyptian University students to "help us get out of the vast prisons we are in . . . just as you helped us to get out on bail from the small prison we were in."

Shortly afterward they were told that they were free to leave Egypt and were given travel documents enabling them to return to Beirut. But at the last moment the Egyptian judiciary—which still retains a measure of independence—refused to allow Monzer Khalifa, the blood drinker, and Essat Rabah, the triggerman, to leave. While their two companions have returned to Beirut to "carry on the fight," Khalifa and Rabah lead a comfortable, boring life in Cairo. Occasionally they even go back to the Sheraton and there, on their way to the Casino to gamble with President Qaddafi's money, they walk over the spot where Wasfi Tell died.

But the story has not yet ended. In April 1973 a Datsun sedan parked in a residential area of Beirut popular with Palestinians was blown into pieces of shredded metal. Nobody was in the car and the explosion seemed a pointless act—the car's owner was involved in neither politics nor crime—until it became known that a similar Datsun, parked nearby, was owned by Ziad Helou, one of the released assassins of Wasfi Tell. It is assumed that the bomb was meant for him and that it was a Jordanian revenge squad that planted it. Certainly Helou thinks so, and in a strange twist of circumstances he has demanded that the Lebanese government protect him from "acts of sabotage by the Jordanian, American and Israeli intelligence departments."

His predicament is common to all who embark on a course of terror. The Islamic vow of "AL AIN BEL AIN AL SEN BEL SEN," an eye for an eye, a tooth for a tooth, is binding on both sides. Hassan el Banna, Supreme Guide of the Moslem Brotherhood, was himself assassinated in 1949 soon after his men had struck down Nokrashy Pasha, the Prime Minister of Egypt, and his successors brought about the destruction of the Brotherhood by their bungled attempt on the life of Nasser. Haj Amin el Husseini, who always wears a bullet-proof jacket under his robes and surrounds himself with armed guards, has survived, but all he has schemed and killed for has been destroyed. "It was the Husseinis who directed the political strategy of the Palestianians until 1947," wrote Professor Elie Kedourie, "and they led them to utter ruin." As for the sixth and last Old Man of the Mountain, he made the grave error of killing a Mongol general at the time when the Mongols were sweeping through the Middle East and the Assassins' power had waned. The Mongols laid siege to his castles, he was captured and sent, a prisoner, to the Great Khan and was never seen again.

Their stories are done, but those of their descendants, the various Arab terrorist organizations, continue, as they began, in bloodshed and violence.

The announcement that Wasfi Tell had been killed by members of a new organization of revenge took most people by surprise even the Israelis. They tended to regard Black September as a group of young hotheads determined to kill King Hussein and his supporters in a purely Jordanian feud. So, for that matter, did Hussein. This opinion was reinforced less than three weeks after Tell's death and when Zaid el Rifai, the Jordanian Ambassador in London and one of Hussein's staunchest supporters, was ambushed as he drove along one of the quite, wealthy streets of Kensington in his ambassadorial Daimler on his way to the Jordanian Embassy in Campden Hill.

A young man loitering on a traffic island at the junction of Campden Hill Road and Duchess of Bedford's Walk aroused the curiosity of William Parsons, an Electricity Board Worker who was carrying out cable repairs, for, as Mr. Parsons pointed out, who wants to loiter on a traffic island? As the Daimler approached, said Mr. Parsons, "I saw the young man pull a Sten gun from under his raincoat. I couldn't believe it. He leveled it at hip height, pulled the trigger, and loosed off about thirty rounds. It was like a scene from a Chicago gangster film."

Bullets riddled the car and one of the first hit el Rifai in the right hand, shattering nearly every bone in it. The Ambassador threw himself on the floor as bullets continued to stitch their way through the bodywork and he shouted at his chauffeur to drive on. The engine stalled for a moment. "It seemed a lifetime," said the Ambassador later. But then it picked up, and el Rifai, blood streaming from his shattered hand, was driven to safety.

The gunman ran down Holland Street and jumped into a red Hillman Hunter which was waiting with its engine running. He and the driver got clean away and were never caught, although Scotland Yard eventually asked the French authorities to deport an Arab they were holding in custody.

He was an Algerian, Frazeh Khelfa, alias Khelfa Same, who was arrested in Lyons in January 1972. The court in Lyons recommended that he be deported to London on a warrant charging him with attempted murder, but the French Ministry of Foreign Affairs, determined to avoid any trouble, released him on a technicality and he slipped out of the country and returned to Algeria.

In Beirut, Black September immediately claimed responsibility for the assassination attempt. Rifai, said their announcement, was No. 3 on its death list after Hussein and Wasfi Tell.

By then Black September's evocative name and its evident ruthlessness had caught the world's imagination, but it was still clothed in mystery. Only its name, it ruthlessness, and its desire for revenge against Hussein and his men were common knowledge. The Palestinian commando organization denied all knowledge of the new group. Few Arabs knew anything about it and those that did were not prepared to talk. But gradually, as Black September's coups grew more melodramatic and more dangerous to the rest of the world, foreign correspondents and the intelligence services of the West began to piece together its story, until today its origins can be traced step by step in a logical progress.

The story starts with the destruction of the Mufti of Jerusalem's forces and the humiliation of the Arab armies in the first Arab-Israeli war of 1947–48. That war left Jordan's British-officered Arab Legion as the only viable fighting force in the Arab world. It also left nearly 600,000 Palestinians homeless and full of hate—not only for the Israelis, who had driven them out of their land, but for their leaders, who had taken them into a war and then deserted them. They were forced to eke out a wretched existence, living on charity in their squalid camps in the Arab lands surrounding Israel.

Nobody wanted them. They were outcasts, and although they could have been absorbed easily into the vast Arab lands surrounding the tiny state of Israel, they were deliberately kept in misery in the camps. There were two main reasons for this policy. The first was that they were feared because on average they were brighter and harder-working than the people in the other Arab countries. And the second was that if they had been absorbed the main reason for the continued enmity against Israel would have been removed, for who could attack the Israelis for being beastly to the Palestinians if the Palestinians were happily and profitably established in the other Arab countries? Instead they were confined to the camps to provide an excuse for those who were determined to destroy Israel, and to justify that destruction by setting before the world a continuing horror show of Israeli brutality. The refugees, who were already full of hatred because of the loss of their homes and their land, were made even more bitter by the conditions of their camps—conditions imposed largely by their brother Arabs.

There was little for them to do except dream of revenge, and gradually they began to band themselves together in a number of organizations under new leaders not tainted with the past. They were kept under strict control by their host countries—nobody wanted to give the Israelis a reason for mounting an attack. But at the same time the Palestinians had to be allowed to undertake certain small operations in order to focus their hatred against the Israelis and not against the countries in which their camps were established.

Egypt's refugee camps were concentrated in the Gaza Strip, the narrow neck of land that runs along the Sinai coast like a pistol pointing at Tel Aviv. Neither Farouk nor Nasser wanted them in Egypt proper. But from Gaza the Palestinians could make their small forays into Israel. They really were small forays.

Quite often a man who had lived close to the border would make his way through the barbed wire just to look at what remained of his house and fields. Other expeditions were less innocent. Water pumps were blown up, cattle slaughtered, crops burned, and sometimes an Israeli settler would be left murdered when the raiders slipped back across the border.

The Israelis, exasperated by these raids, retaliated with a punitive attack on the Egyptian army headquarters in the Gaza Strip on the night of February 28, 1955, which left thirty-eight people dead. In face of this attack and the demands for revenge from the Egyptian army and the Palestinians, President Nasser ordered the training, arming and unleashing of the Palestinian fedayeen on sabotage and guerrilla operations inside Israeli territory. It was a dire mistake on Nasser's part, for it gave the Israelis the excuse they wanted to attack Egypt in the second round of the Arab-Israeli conflict, the Suez Affair of 1956.

In the aftermath of those battles, in which the Israelis, with the help of the French and British, inflicted another defeat on the Egyptian army, a number of fighting groups were organized among the Palestinians. These groups acted independently, relying for arms and patronage on the various Arab countries in which they made their headquarters. Among these organizations was one called Al Fatah, a name formed from a play on the reversed initials of the Palestine Liberation Movement and meaning Victory. Read the right way round the initials would have read Hataf, which means Death. Fatah had a military wing called el Assifa, the Storm, and it was run by a pudgy schoolteacher called Yasir Arafat, who was unknown outside the fedayeen movement.

None of these groups was important until January 1964, when, at the first Arab summit meeting in Cairo, Ahmed Shukairy, a verbose diplomat and lawyer who had just been appointed the Palestinian representative on the Arab League Council, suggested to Nasser that a Palestinian national entity should be organized in exile.

Nasser, who saw the opportunity of displaying his support for the Palestinian cause without giving Israel dangerous offense, readily accepted this suggestion and pushed the other Arab leaders into accepting Shukairy's proposal. But Shukairy, an ambitious man, was not content with the mere acceptance of his plan. He wanted something concrete, and so he called a Palestine Congress which met in Jerusalem four months later and at his urging formed the Palestine Liberation Organization. The PLO was designed to provide a framework within which all the Palestinian activist groups could work and would in fact act as a government in exile—with Shukairy at its head. At the second Arab summit meeting in Alexandria that September, the decision was taken to provide the PLO with a military arm, the Palestine Liberation Army. Six million Egyptian pounds were allocated for its establishment and the Arab leaders committed themselves to paying shares in its budget. Nasser showed tremendous enthusiasm. The army was to be quartered in Gaza, trained by regular Egyptian army instructors and given arms from Egyptian arsenals. It was also to be kept on a very short rein by the Egyptians.

Not all the Arab leaders were as enthusiastic as Nasser. The Syrians, in particular, disliked the way the PLO and its army appeared to be a completely Egyptian affair with Nasser gaining all the credit. And so the Syrians decided to support their own band of guerrillas. They chose the little-known Fatah group, which, since it was set up in 1956 by Arafat, had spent most of its time organizing itself into commands and undercover cells. It had undertaken a few raids out of the Gaza Strip but had accomplished little.

However, under Syrian patronage, Arafat and his men were provided with training grounds close to the Israeli border, given weapons and encouraged to raid across the border into the lush but vulnerable farmland of northern Israel. The Syrians encouraged Fatah in its campaign of violence but took care that most of the raids were mounted across the Jordanian border so that the inevitable Israeli reaction was aimed at Jordan and not at Syria. Nevertheless the Syrians gained great credit in the Arab world for their activism, which was compared critically with the inactivity of the Egyptians. Virtually the only show of force Nasser allowed the PLA was Ahmed Shukairy's blood-curdling speeches.

The Syrians were delighted by this state of affairs and urged Arafat into undertaking more and more forays. Mines were laid, farms shot up, reservoirs sabotaged. During April and May of 1967 hardly a day passed without Fatah carrying out some act of violence. The Israeli leaders replied with threatening speeches which were construed as an indication that the Israeli army was about to march on Damascus and overthrow the government. The Syrians panicked, appealed to Nasser for help and he was forced to march his army into the Sinai to show his solidarity with his Arab brothers—who were in fact his bitter rivals. From that act stemmed the closing of the Gulf of Aqaba to Israeli shipping, which made an Israeli attack on Egypt inevitable and so precipitated the third Arab-Israeli war, the Six Day War of June 1967. It destroyed the armies of Egypt, Jordan and Syria and sent a further 150,000 Palestinians to the refugee camps and, in the continuing escalation of killing in the Middle East, set the scene for the terror to come.

This is necessarily a short account of the events leading up to the Six Day War and there were many other factors involved, but there is no doubt that Arafat and his men carry a good deal of the blame for bringing that war about. Their responsibility is equal to that of Haj Amin's for bringing about the Arab disaster in 1948. But whereas the Mufti was broken, Arafat and Fatah emerged from the Six Day War more powerful than ever.

While the Arab armies were incapable of mounting any form of resistance to the Israelis under the shock of total defeat, Arafat started a series of guerrilla operations inside Israel and the newly occupied territories. In July 1967 he slipped into Jerusalem, his home town, and set up Fatah cells there and in Nablus. The Israelis almost caught him. They learned that he was staying at a house in Nablus, surrounded it and demanded his surrender. But the old matriarch who opened the door to the Israelis led them instead to her own son, who pretended to be Arafat, was arrested and taken away to prison while the real Arafat made good his escape. He returned to Damascus, dismissed all idea of political action and concentrated on sabotage activities against Israel. Nasser looked on these activities as "one of the most healthy phenomena that came directly after defeat." Arafat in turn began to come more and more under Nasser's influence. His own prestige grew. He was appointed leader to the PLO in place of Shukairy. And he made contacts with other Arab countries in order to procure arms and money. The oil-rich states were happy to subsidize him with conscience money for not having taken part in the war.

His forces, swollen now by the fresh flood of refugees and the prestige he had gained—more from the flamboyant communiqués he put out rather than solid military successes—grouped in Jordan. King Hussein was unable to prevent them setting up a virtually autonomous state inside the borders of his truncated kingdom. The Palestinians are the Jews of the Arab world. They are clever, technical-minded people and were first welcomed into Jordan by King Abdullah to provide the civil servants and technicians needed to run his country, for his people were largely desert Bedouins who, while they were fierce warriors and completely loyal to the royal family, lacked the desire and the ability to staff the ministries in Amman. These displaced Palestinians occupied, and many of them still occupy, high posts in the Jordanian government and the army and to them Fatah's presence provided the one light in the darkness of defeat that shrouded all Arabia.

In order to understand the events that follow one must first realize how deep that darkness was and the agony of shame and despair that filled every Arab's heart after June 1967.

The Arabs are a proud people who, in the seventh century, afire with the faith of the Prophet Mohammed, burst out of the Arabian Peninsula on their war camels and built an empire that ran from Spain to Mongolia and but for the defeat they suffered at the Battle of Poitiers in 732 would have marched on Paris. They built a remarkable civilization, introducing scientific irrigation to Europe, inventing algebra, studying the movements of the stars. They undertook great voyages of exploration. Baghdad became a center of medieval culture. Their architecture remains one of the glories of Spain. And the wealth and luxury of their courts has not been equaled in the Middle East until today, when the riches brought by oil have enabled the desert sheiks to live once again like Haroun al Rashid, the most splendid of the Caliphs of Baghdad, who truly lived in the style of the *Thousand and One Nights*. Silk from Samarkand, carpets from Bokhara, jewels from India, exotic fruits and spices from the East Indies, swords and damask from Damascus, furs from Russia, the finest products of craftsmanship filled Arabia. Philosophers and mathematicians, poets and singers, astronomers and writers, doctors and historians, all flourished in this golden age. It was a civilization of such refinement, learning and chivalry that it astonished the rough Crusader knights when they invaded the Holy Land from their rude castles in the cold north. These knights, with their chain mail, their huge two-handed swords and their illiterate peasant soldiers rode out of the Dark Ages into the warmth and light of the Middle East to attack a civilization they called "infidel" which was far more advanced in learning, organization and religious tolerance than their own. The war between the Arabs and the Crusaders lasted for some two hundred years before the Christians were finally and bloodily thrown out of the Holy Land. But by now the Mongols were on the march. Tamerlane swept through Syria and built a grisly pyramid of the skulls of twenty thousand of Aleppo's citizens. The great Arab civilization crumbled, and when the Mongols retreated the Turks spread along the Mediterranean, occupying the Arabs' lands until only the inaccessible heartland of the Arabian Peninsula, from which the Arab conquerors had exploded nine hundred years before, was left to them, and the Arabs lapsed into impotence, poverty and ignorance. This period came to be known as "the Sleep of Ages" and was to last three hundred years until Napoleon arrived in Cairo with his army and his retinue of scholars. He remained for only one year, but the Pharaonic discoveries of his intellectuals not only aroused worldwide interest in the ancient civilization of Egypt, they also aroused the Arabs from their sleep, made them aware of their glorious past and long for an equally glorious future. But they had sunk deep in sloth and squalor. There was nothing in the whole of the Arab world which could compare with the glories of the past. They were occupied countries. The British had Egypt and the Turks had the rest, and even when the Turks were driven out during World War I in a campaign which owed much to the desert warriors who had never been conquered, they were denied their independence, with the British and the French carving up the Arab lands between them. There was little of the pride and chivalry of the great Saladin, who had led them to victory against the Crusaders, left in the average Arab. They were despised as "wogs" by the British army in both World Wars, they were thought of as sellers of dirty postcards and whore-mongers who would sell their own sisters. And their bitterness was great.

On top of all this humiliation they saw the great wealth of the oil fields which they regarded as their birthright going into the pockets of the Western oil companies and a few feudal sheiks, and they saw a Jewish state set up in the very land for which their ancestors had fought the Crusaders for so many years. The British and French, hard-pressed in World War I, had made promises to the Arabs in return for their assistance in defeating "Johnny Turk," and they had gone to war under the romantic Lawrence of Arabia believing that these promises meant complete independence for the Arabs once the war was won. But the British and the French had their own plans; they had not only agreed to carve up the Middle East between them, they had set out to insure the support of the world's powerful Jewish communities. And they had done this by promising to set up a national home for the Jews in the very country that the Arabs believed had been promised to them. This promise to the Zionists, the men who were working for the return of the Jews to the homeland from which they had been driven by the Romans two thousand years before, was contained in one of history's most fateful documents, the Balfour Declaration of November 2, 1917. This declaration was in fact a 117-word note written to Lord Rothschild, head of the British branch of the Jewish banking family, in which Lloyd George's Foreign Secretary, Arthur Balfour, said:

Dear Lord Rothschild.

I have much pleasure in conveying to you, on behalf of His Majesty's Government, the following declaration of sympathy with Jewish Zionist aspirations which has been submitted to and approved by the Cabinet.

"His Majesty's Government view with favor the establishment in Palestine of a national home for the Jewish people, and will use their best endeavors to facilitate the achievement of this object, it being clearly undersood that nothing shall be done which may prejudice the civil and religious rights of existing non-Jewish communities in Palestine, or the rights and political status enjoyed by Jews in any other country."

I should be grateful if you would bring this declaration to the knowledge of the Zionist Federation.

Yours sincerely,
Arthur James Balfour

The Zionists reacted with joy to the Declaration, but a few days after it was published the young David Ben Gurion wrote an article in a New York weekly in which he said: "England has not given us back the Land of Israel. It is at this very moment, when we feel joy at the the great victory, that we must make it very clear: England cannot give us back the Land of Israel. This is not because the country is not, or not yet, under her control. Even after England exercises sovereignty over the entire Land of Israel, from Beersheba to Dan, it will not become ours simply because that is her desire, not even if all the other countries of the world agree as well. A land can be won by a people only through their own efforts and creativity, their building and settlement.

"England has done a great deal: She has recognized our existence as a political entity and our right to the country. The Jewish people must now transform this recognition into a living reality, by investing their strength, spirit, energy and capital in building a National Home and achieving full national salvation."

To the Arabs the Balfour Declaration was a base betrayal. It meant to them that their land was being given to an alien people and they feared precisely what Ben Gurion was advocating, that the "strength, spirit, energy and capital" of the Jews would be employed in building a state of Israel from Beersheba to Dan.

It took another thirty years before this was to come about and it succeeded only then because of the pressure of the survivors of Hitler's holocaust.

The Arabs tried to snuff out the life of the newborn state in 1948 and were humiliated. They were thrashed again in 1956 when the Israelis joined with Britain and France in the Suez adventure. And then came the June War of 1967. It opened to the boasts of the Arab leaders that Israel was about to be destroyed. It ended six days later with the destruction of the armies of Egypt, Jordan and Syria. It was after this stunning victory that President de Gaulle created a furor by describing the Jewish people as "an elite, self-assured and domineering."

The Israelis, supersensitive to any hint of anti-Semitism, objected violently to this description. They might have reflected that there was a paradox and a warning involved, because the Arabs, in their golden age had been "an elite, self-assured and domineering," were now abject, wallowing in self-pity and shame.

And so in 1967 all Arabs looked toward the little spark of defiance shown by Fatah as a symbol of hope and pride. The Jordanian terrain was ideal for guerrilla training and bases, and the long border along the river Jordan was open to Fatah's raiding parties, while fighting cells in the Gaza Strip and the West Bank carried out their own operations. The operations were small and the communiqués which followed them were so bombastic and so obviously untrue that the Israelis were able to dismiss them as useless. In military terms the Israelis were correct. They killed or captured a high proportion of the guerrillas who came across the Jordan and an equally high proportion of the fedayeen found the going so rough they would set off their explosive charges and fire their guns on their own side of the Jordan and then return to base claiming a great victory against the Israeli army. However, they did hurt the Israelis and it was mainly the Israelis' own fault, for there is a tradition in the Israeli army of officers leading from the front with the cry: "Follow me." This is fine in open warfare, but when employed against two or three guerrillas holed up in a cave it proved much too expensive, with a number of high-ranking officers being killed on minor operations. The Israeli authorities became increasingly disturbed by the Fatah operations and in early 1968 it became obvious that they would soon mount a punitive expedition. The incident that set the expedition in motion came on March 18, when a bus carrying schoolchildren from Tel Aviv on a trip to the Negev desert was blown up by a Fatah mine. Two of the children were killed and twenty-eight were wounded. The seriousness of this incident must not be underestimated, for it must be remembered that it was the fedayeen attacks from Gaza which provoked the Israeli attack on Egypt in 1956 and it was the activities of Fatah on the Syrian border which set the scene for the Six Day War.

This time the Israelis sent two columns of tanks and half-tracks with artillery and air support to attack the Fatah base in the Jordanian village of Karameh, which means Dignity. The Israelis insist that this was not a punitive raid but was a pre-emptive strike designed to prevent a large-scale campaign of terror planned by Fatah. Whatever the reason, they were determined to wipe out Karameh. The operation was, however, out of the usual Israeli context. There was no sudden, damn-the-consequence assault. Instead, the Jordanians were warned beforehand not to interfere, leaflets were dropped to the villagers telling them they would not be harmed and the raiding troops were given strict orders not to harm civilians or to fire at houses unless they were fired on.

Whether this was because the Israelis had become over-confident or had become sensitive to world opinion is not clear, but what is clear is that the warnings they gave insured that they were met not by an enemy disorganized by surprise but one prepared for the attack and very willing to fight. The Battle of Karameh on March 21, 1968, proved a turning point in Fatah's history because the young commandos fought bravely and effectively against the vaunted Israelis. They fought from house to house, with teen-agers hurling themselves against the Israeli tanks. They killed twenty-nine Israelis and wounded seventy, but in the end the battle-hardened Israelis got the upper hand, blowing up the fortified houses, killing a hundred and fifty guerrillas and capturing as many again. The rest of the Fatah force was saved from annihilation only by the arrival of a Jordanian armored column. The Israelis were surprised by this intervention, thinking that the Jordanians would be as anxious as they were to see the fedayeen wiped out, and broke off the engagement. Immediately, the guerrillas, ignoring their losses and the Jordanian intervention, claimed a glorious victory. The news rang round the Arab world and its effect was astonishing. The Arabs had lived on a diet of defeat for so long it had seemed that no Arab force could stand up to the Israeli army, and now, suddenly, they were told that a small band armed only with grenades and assault rifles had defeated a task force of Israeli tanks and planes. That this was not strictly true did not matter. The Battle of Karamah cannot be measured in military terms. It had demonstrated that the Israelis were not invincible and it became a symbol of hope for the Arabs.

Arafat and Fatah became heroes. Recruits and weapons and money poured in. The fedayeen grew bold. They swaggered through Jordan with their new Russian weapons and, although they still achieved little of military value inside Israel, their propaganda turned their small successes into massive victories. The period from 1968 to 1969 was the Golden Era of the Palestinian resistance movement.

During this same period Nasser's Russian-built missile boats sank the Israeli destroyer *Elath* and he started the War of Attrition across the Suez Canal. Arab guns were firing again. The prospect of regaining the lost land of Palestine seemed no longer a dream to the Arabs, whose character it is to soar on the wings of wishes from the deepest pit of despair to the most dangerous peaks of overconfidence.

But while they were happily contemplating that prospect the forces of further disaster were already at work. Unity is an ephemeral phenomenon in the Arab world; alliances are made and broken overnight. Seemingly fast friends become enemies, and enemies, friends. And so it was with the Palestinian resistance movement. The seemingly solid front was only a façade; behind it the body of the movement was breaking apart into rival factions. Fatah was committed to a military struggle against Israel. The Popular Front for the Liberation of Palestine, led by Dr. George Habash, dedicated itself to world revolution and spurned the idea of a military confrontation with the Israelis. They went underground—and so saved themselves from the catastrophe that was about to strike the guerrillas. The PFLP developed its own divisive force, the Popular Democratic Front for the Liberation of Palestine, under the leadership of the Maoist Naif Hawatmeh, and he and his two hundred followers claim that they are the only pure revolutionaries among the Arabs. El Saiqa, the Thunderbolt, was organized by the Syrian ruling Ba'ath party to counteract Egypt's influence over Fatah, and the Arab Liberation Front was sponsored by the Iraqi Ba'ath party for the same reason. With all these rivalries at work there was no united effort. The fedayeen were also now taking heavy casualities from Israeli counter-guerrilla forces. The small groups operating inside Israel were wiped out one by one, the raiding forays across the Jordan began to take on the character of suicide missions and in the Gaza Strip the Israeli army ruled the Arab population under strict military law; indeed, while unwary Israelis driving through Gaza with their car windows rolled down occasionally found grenades in their laps, most of the casualties in the Strip were Arabs, killed by other Arabs to discourage collaboration with the Israeli authorities. Israeli figures show that in the four years from the middle of 1967 to the middle of 1971 the fedayeen operating in Gaza killed 138 of their brother Arabs and wounded 1,119.

Israeli army pressure forced the commandos to change their tactics. They now sought to avoid combat and concentrated on long-range attacks with Russian and Chinese Katyusha rockets on the northern towns and kibbutzim, and bazooka and machine-gun ambushes across the river Jordan. The rocket attacks in the north were quite effective. The Katyushas would be set up in the desolate, rocky hills inside the Lebanese border, aimed at towns such as Kiryat Shemona. They were fitted with time fuses, so that the rocketeers would be miles away when their missiles went crashing into the sleeping settlements. Many of the inhabitants of this part of Israel are Oriental Jews who, over the years, have absorbed the Arab attitudes of the countries in which they lived and were consequently not as well endowed with martial fervor as the Jews from Western Europe. And so, for a time, there was a crisis of morale in the communities north of Galilee. One particular incident caused both outrage and fear. A school bus being driven along the road that marks the border with Lebanon was hit by remote-controlled missiles and twelve of the passengers, including eight children, were killed. The world was horrified, but many Israelis were terrified and there was something of an exodus from the north. This was probably the only real success in terms of disruption of daily life—outside Gaza—that the commandos could legitimately claim. The Israelis reacted by raiding deeper and deeper into Lebanon in search-and-destroy operations, a tactic which was to have a major effect on the Middle East situation.

The ambushes across the Jordan were contained by an intricate system of patrols behind the barbed wire and minefields that line the river. I set out with one of these patrols before dawn one summer's day in 1970. The soldiers, Druse tribesmen who had joined the Frontier Force, rumbled off from their barracks in Beth Shean, the city to whose wall the Philistines fastened the body of King Saul after they had killed him on Mount Gilboa. These modern warriors rode in Russian armored trucks which had been captured during the 1967 war.

Each truck bristled with weapons, a .50-caliber machine gun, a light machine gun, a mortar and the patrol's individual weapons. The one I rode in had a curious sort of armored seat welded onto a long arm sticking out in front of the truck's hood. This, I was told, was the seat of honor, where a member of the patrol sat and searched for mines as the truck drove slowly along the frontier roads. The patrol's job was to sweep the road clear of mines and ambushes so that the kibbutz farmers could till their fields in comparative safety. We reached the rendezvous point just as the sun was coming up out of Jordan. It was still cool. The light was clear, and the dawn chorus magnificent. Behind us were the burnt brown hills of the Israeli side of the Jordan Valley sloping down to the cotton and corn fields of the farmers. The Jordanian hills loomed on the other side, and beneath them were the fields of the Arab farmers. A tank rattled past. A startled hare dashed for safety and the soldiers checked their weapons.

Part of the patrol set out on foot to check the paths along the river while the trucks took up covering positions. We were strung out ten yards apart. It was ideal country for an ambush, with dried up wadis, little hills and long grass giving excellent cover. I was uncomfortably aware that just across the sweet flowing river where fish were rising to the morning hatch of flies there were eyes watching every step I took. It began to get hot. Burdened with a steel helmet and a flak jacket, I began to sweat. But there was nothing to be seen. The sandy track was bare of the footprints that would indicate a mining party had slipped across during the night; the only tracks were those of snakes. We walked for an hour. I was soaked with sweat and the Jordan ran invitingly, playing cool music on the rocks. We marched on.

Then we met up with the truck. Tension eased. Somebody lit a cigarette. I watched the birds, brilliant bee eaters, partridge, quail, larks and turtle doves. Suddenly there was a burst of machine-gun fire, then a crackle on the radio. The patrol from the next truck had been ambushed. One man had been hit. Everybody piled into the truck and we drove off to help. The big machine gun whose shells can tear a man in half searched out the ambushers.

Other trucks joined in. The fedayeen returned the fire. Everyone opened up. Soon the floor of the truck was littered with spent cartridge cases. The artillery joined in and a tank moved up to join in the fray. The little battle lasted for ten minutes. At the end of it one Druse was dead and the Israelis claimed they had seen one of the fedayeen fall. As we drove back to breakfast the farmers were already working in their fields. It had been a fairly normal start to the day.

As it happened, this was one of the last of the Jordan River ambushes, for on July 23, 1970, Nasser accepted the cease-fire proposed by U.S. Secretary of State William Rogers. The guns fell silent along the Suez, but their silence was matched by the howls of rage from the Syrians, the Iraqis and the Palestinians, who accused Nasser of betraying the Liberation movement—although the Syrians and the Iraqis took care not to involve themselves in the fight. Many of the fedayeen saw no further point in risking their own necks if Nasser was not prepared to fight and so they began to slip quietly away to a more peaceful life.

The Rogers Plan is blamed by many Arabs as the starting point of the decline of the true military resistance movement. But something far more dramatic was about to happen which would mark the end of Fatah's ability to wage war and lead directly to the birth of Black September.

The Popular Front for the Liberation of Palestine, having rejected Arafat's theory of military resistance, had turned to terror for its weapon to strike at the Israelis and their American supporters. They started with the hijacking of an El Al Boeing 707 on its way from Rome to Lod airport on July 23, 1968. They forced the pilot to land in Algiers, where the Israelis on board were imprisoned for two months. On December 26 of that same year a PFLP group armed with submachine guns opened up on another El Al Boeing as it took off from Athens airport, killing a passenger and wounding a stewardess. The PFLP group was arrested by the Greek police. The attack and the arrests had two results. The arrests led to a further hijacking to secure the release of the terrorists and this has now become standard procedure whenever a terrorist is arrested. It also led to a retaliatory attack by Israeli helicopter-borne troops on Beirut airport, which left thirteen Arab airliners smoking wrecks on the tarmac. The raid was brilliantly planned and ruthlessly carried out and its purpose was to convince the Lebanese that they were responsible for acts carried out by terrorists based on their territory and that they had better control the terrorists—or else. The raid caused a worldwide debate on the question of its justification. The Israelis were criticized for exacting too massive a revenge. But they took no notice of the criticism. They made it clear they would strike back whenever they were attacked and that their attacks would include the terrorists' host countries. It is said that the Lebanese were not too disturbed by the raid, because the insurance for their wrecked airliners enabled them to replace their aging planes with a brand-new fleet. But they took note of the Israeli warning and took some steps to try to curb anti-Israeli activities—at least those that could be traced back to Lebanon. Hussein, too, took note of the warning. He was already concerned with the way in which Fatah seemed to be taking over Jordan and he tried to enforce a ruling that only members of the armed forces could carry arms in public, but this led to clashes which cost several hundred lives and Hussein was forced to dismiss two of his generals in exchange for an agreement which was obviously made to be broken. Arafat also took note of the PFLP terrorism and was critical of it because he felt it would give the world a wrong image of the Arab cause. The only people who were unconcerned were George Habash, his second in command, Wadi Haddad, and their fanatical followers. They carried out attacks on El Al offices in Athens, Brussels, Berlin, Teheran and Istanbul. They blew up a Swissair plane in mid-air on its way to Tel Aviv, killing forty-seven people. They killed seven old people by setting fire to the Jewish Home for the Aged in Munich. They hijacked a Lufthansa Jumbo jet and forced it to land in Aden. They threw a grenade at an airline bus in Munich and tore the leg off one of Israel's best-loved actresses, Hannah Marron. This catalogue of terror rolled on with two or three incidents every month and nearly every one of them was the work of PFLP.

When the Italian journalist Oriana Fallaci interviewed George Habash and pointed out that his acts of terrorism had killed many innocent people, the PFLP displayed the twisted thinking that was to become the justification for every act of Arab terror. It is a terrifying example of how any action, however ruthless, can be made to seem logical and just. "Non-Israeli passengers," said Habash, "are on their way to Israel. Since we have no control over the land that was stolen from us and called Israel, it is right that whoever goes to Israel should ask for our permission. . . . Our struggle has barely begun, the worst is yet to come. And it is right for Europe and America to be warned now that there will be no peace until there is justice for Palestine. . . . The prospect of triggering a third World War doesn't bother us. The world has been using us and has forgotten us. It is time they realized we exist, it is time they stopped exploiting us. Whatever the price, we'll continue our struggle. . . . We are the joker in the pack. Without our consent the other Arabs can do nothing. And we will never agree to a peaceful settlement. If the Arab countries think they can gang up and make peace over our heads, they are mistaken. All we have to do is to assert our power in one country and the rest will lose their resolve and start backsliding. . . ."

This cruel arrogance led the PFLP to launch the biggest and most daring hijack operation of all time. On September 6, 1970, four jet airliners were attacked. Two of them, belonging to TWA and Swissair, were flown to Dawson's Field, a wartime RAF airfield in the wilds of the Jordanian desert where the pilots made hair-raising landings on long-disused runways and where the crews and passengers were made hostage. A third plane, belonging to Pan American, was forced to fly to Cairo, where, after the passengers and crew had escaped down the crash chutes, the plane was blown up by explosives planted by the terrorists. Only the fourth attempt failed, and this was the one that became the most famous because it was carried out by the girl terrorist Leila Khaled and the international revolutionary Patrick Arguello. It failed because after the first successful hijacking of the El Al Boeing, the Israeli authorities had adopted the most stringent precautions. They had flown a Boeing 707 over the Negev desert and exploded grenades inside the fuselage to determine how much punishment the aircraft could take. They had installed armored doors between the flight deck and the passenger compartment. And they had set up the '007 Squad," a group of specially trained young men, most of them paratroopers, to guard the plane in the air. These guards are equipped with .22 pistols, which can kill but do not go through a human body with enough velocity to harm a plane's pressurized hull. They have orders never to surrender to hijackers. They must always fight it out. And that is what they did when Leila made her try over the English Channel. She almost succeeded because the "007 Squad" was caught off guard. They had been tipped off that a hijacking was possible, but when they heard over the aircraft's radio of one of the other hijackings, they relaxed, not considering the possibility that they were part of a multiple coup. However, they recovered in time to kill Arguello, a Nicaraguan-American, and to capture Leila Khaled. El Al pilots have instructions that they must fly directly back to Israel in hijack situations. But Captain Uri Bar-Lev ignored that instruction and landed at London's Heathrow Airport because Shlomo Vider, one of his stewards, who had tackled Arguello, had been shot no less than five times by the terrorist and needed urgent hospital treatment. This action by Bar-Lev was to have quite unforeseen results. The Shin Bet, the Israeli Department of Internal Security, was furious with him, for Leila Khaled was one of its principal targets. Bar-Lev flew home to a muted welcome and was grounded for a month.

Leila, meanwhile, was under lock and key in Ealing police station. But not for long. Three days later a BOAC VC-10 was hijacked on its way from Bahrain to London in order to provide hostages for Leila's release and it joined the other two airlines at Dawson's Field.

There were now 425 people sweltering inside the three planes in the fearsome desert heat under threat of being blown up if the world did not give in to the terrorists' demands. Those demands were simple: they wanted the release of Leila Khaled, three PFLP members held in West Germany for the attack on the airline bus at Munich, three more held by the Swiss for shooting up an El Al plane at Zurich and killing the copilot and an unspecified number of fedayeen held by the Israelis. If not, said the terrorists, then the planes and people in them would be blown up at precisely three o'clock on the morning of Thursday, September 10.

It is probable that while these demands were very real the ultimate objective of the PFLP—and it seems that at this time the organization was being run by Wadi Haddad, for George Habash was in North Korea—was to provoke a situation which would wreck the cease-fire and bring Israel and Egypt into conflict again in the hope that the cause of extremism would gain advantage from the inevitable chaos. It certainly provoked a conflict, but not the expected one. For while protracted negotiations were going on for the release of the hostages—most of them were released, but forty were kept imprisoned in a refugee camp in Amman after the terrorists had blown up the airliners—King Hussein, infuriated by the PFLP's misuse of his country and under enormous pressure from his army to bring the guerrillas under control, finally unleashed his Bedouin soldiers against the commandos they had grown to hate.

Hussein told a correspondent from *Le Figaro* that his army had had enough, "they are not accustomed to being so vilified, denigrated and provoked endlessly without being able to react." And he spoke bitterly of asking one tank commander why he had a brassiere flying from his radio antenna, and of the soldier replying, "Because we are women."

Hussein's assault took in not only the PFLP but also Fatah. There was a dreadful slaughter, in the course of which the remaining hijack hostages were rescued. The refugee camps were shelled. The Bedouin, enraged by the arrogance of Fatah, gave no quarter and killed some four thousand of the fedayeen. The Syrians tried to intervene by sending in a brigade of tanks and claiming that they belonged to the Palestine Liberation Army (PLA), but Hussein's air force dealt with them, and when the fighting ended with a cease-fire imposed by Nasser, the guerrillas' power in Jordan had been broken. It truly was a Black September for them. The effort of making peace, of getting Hussein and Arafat—both wearing revolvers—to sit at the same table killed Nasser and it became obvious that the precarious peace he had engineered could not survive for long.

I do not think it is generally understood just how close the Middle East—and possibly the rest of the world—came to a general conflagration during this inter-Arab fighting. Neither the Israelis nor the Americans would have allowed Hussein to be defeated, and when the Syrians sent in their tanks Israel and the United States made plans to move in and settle the issue. Lieutenant General Haim Bar-Lev, then Chief of Staff of the Israeli army, spelled out the problem as he saw it: "I can visualize a state of deterioration in Jordan or one that is connected with Jordan which would warrant military steps being taken by us. For example, and perhaps the most obvious one: A state of deterioration along our borders, as a result of terrorist activities or a combination of terrorist and regular army activities, would be quite likely to warrant military action on our part—but this would differ in scope and nature from our other activities to date. Should Israel be confronted with a choice between evacuating settlements and civilians from the border, and taking military steps of a serious dimension, I assume that the second choice would be the one taken."

The Americans had already taken action on their own accord. The Sixth Fleet was steaming ostentatiously ninety miles off the Israeli coast. The attack carrier *John F. Kennedy* was hurrying to the scene to add its planes to the Fleet's already awesome amount of power. The Eighth Infantry Division in Germany had been put on standby. Twelve thousand paratroopers based in the United States were prepared to be airlifted. America had enough men and matériel ready to fight a major war.

How close were the Israelis to going into Jordan to stabilize the "state of deterioration" there? I had the good fortune to be in Tel Aviv at the time—most of my colleagues were shut up by the guerrillas in the Intercontinental Hotel in Amman—when the news came of the Syrian tank invasion. So I headed north to the area just below the Sea of Galilee, where Israel, Jordan and Syria meet. It was sweltering hot in the Beisan Valley, where the river Jordan flows down from the Galilee beneath the Gilead Hills. It was from these hills that the Fatah rocketeers had been firing their Katyushas into the kibbutzim on the Israeli side of the river, and the Israelis had no intention of allowing the Syrians to take control of these hills. I stopped the car and looked across the border into Jordan at the sand-colored Arab villages, their houses standing square, with tiny shuttered windows, baking in the sun. But they were ghost villages; the inhabitants had fled when the Israelis bombed them in retaliation for the rocket attacks. They had become terrorist hideouts, but now even the terrorists had gone, into Amman and Ramtha and Irbid to fight the King. Nothing moved over there except the hawks hovering over the neglected fields. The stillness was so complete it was eerie. There was nothing to see except dust devils whirling through the heat haze and an Israeli armored truck patrolling the riverbank. Then I became conscious of a rumbling in the distance. It was muted like distant surf crashing onto rocks, but this noise came out of the burnt, forbidding hills of Jordan and was the sound of a continuous artillery barrage. I headed for the sound of gunfire, but the Israeli army had sealed the frontier roads and no amount of cajolery or flashing of press cards could get me past the road blocks. The closest I got to the war was at Tel Katsir at the toe of the Sea of Galilee, where I sat outside a café owned by the local kibbutz eating steak and chips and listening to the cannonfire rolling round the hills. Israeli jets, shining silver in a burnished blue sky, flashed over the quiet green waters and the kibbutzniks harvested their cotton and plowed the fields for next year's crops. I set out to return to Tel Aviv, tired, hot and rather disappointed. I had something of a story but it was nothing to shout about. Suddenly, in front of the car there appeared three tank transporters carrying Centurion main battle tanks. They turned off the road into a field which had been empty when I passed it that morning. Now it had troops lining up at a canteen, and tucked away among the trees were a squadron of Centurions. I drove slowly along the frontier roads and it soon became obvious that I had run in to the vanguard of an armored task force rolling up toward the frontier. There were more and more tanks, columns of half-tracks carrying recoilless rifles and automatic cannon, communications vehicles and truckloads of fully armed troops. The Israeli army was on the move.

I learned later that if Hussein had not managed to deal with the Syrian tanks, the Israelis would have gone into Jordan and would have had the support of the American forces if it had been militarily necessary. The international consequences of such a move would have been extremely dangerous. There would certainly have been accusations of imperialisim from the Arab states and it is unlikely that Russia could have remained out of the quarrel, for the Soviets had already lost a great deal of prestige in the Middle East for not coming to the aid of the Arabs during the Six Day War. Oil supplies would have been threatened. And the specter of World War conjured up.

In the event, Hussein gave the Syrians what he described as "a bloody nose" and the Israelis packed up and went home and the Americans stood down while Hussein mopped up the guerrillas.

Jordan became dangerous territory for the fedayeen after this defeat and they retreated to Lebanon and Syria. But one of their leaders remained behind and gathered around him the fiercest of the survivors. He was Abu Ali Iyad, a one-eyed fighting man of great ugliness, strength and charisma. He was one of the men who had worked inside Israel with Arafat immediately after the Six Day War and proved to be a born leader. The young fedayeen adored him as a warrior and when, in the summer of 1971, Hussein decided to clear the remnants of the guerrillas out of his kingdom, Abu Ali Iyad gathered his men around him and fought to the end. In July he was wounded and captured in the fighting around Jerash, where the fedayeen made their last stand against Hussein's Bedouins. His followers claim that he was tortured and killed personally by Wasfi Tell. Certainly his body was dragged around the villages behind a tank. His death was a grievous blow to the young men who saw in him a fighting leader to replace Arafat, who they dismissed as a "Grand Hotel revolutionary"—a term of abuse dating from the days of British rule when Arab leaders seemed to do nothing but sit around Grand Hotels. Now he had been killed by the hated Wasfi Tell and so his followers and his relatives, particularly his sister, formed their own small secret society called "The Revenging Palestinians." It was decided to avenge his death by killing Wasfi Tell.

Fatah was in disarray. Many of its leaders and best fighting men had been killed. The remnants had fled from Jordan. They were unwelcome in Egypt. Syria imposed stringent restrictions on their operations. So did Iraq. Lebanon was the only country with access to Israel which was also weak enough to be unable to prevent them setting up shop. They were given control of fifteen refugee camps in Lebanon, but the Lebanese army tried to confine them to training camps and tactical bases in the Arkoub, a desolate area in the southeast corner of the country bordering on Israel, from where they continued to launch their Katyushas against the Israeli settlements. The Israelis responded in their normal fashion with heavy punitive raids into Lebanon designed not only to kill fedayeen but also to convince the Lebanese that they must curb the guerrillas' activities.

Fatah came under pressure from all sides. It was paid protection money by the rich oil states. Its men were trained in Egypt and Libya and Algeria. A flood of words was set flowing on its behalf. But nothing active was done to restore the commando's military power. Instead, restraint was urged upon them. And so, no longer able to mount military operations, the Palestinians felt their very existence threatened. They were of secondary importance in the traumatic period following Nasser's death when the Arab world was adjusting to the loss of the man who had reflected its hopes and its follies for sixteen years. It seemed that Karameh would be forgotten, Palestine lost forever and Palestinians doomed to be like the Jews two thousand years before, a nation without a country.

It was in this atmosphere of near despair that Fatah's Revolutionary Council met in Damascus in September 1971—a year after the debacle brought upon them by PFLP's terrorism and their own arrogance. As so often happens in the Arab world, this controlling body was hopelessly split. Arafat led the old guard, who, despite their military aspirations of the previous four years, now argued that the Palestinians had never really been a military power and it had been foolish ever to dream of winning back their land in military action against Israel. Their methods had to be political, they said, and they had to be directed at gaining sufficient support to be able to exercise a veto over any Arab country making peace with Israel. They were opposed by the militants of the Revenging Palestinians, who argued that the only course open to them if they wanted to remain in existence was to turn to clandestine activity like the PFLP, using spectacular terrorist coups to make and keep the world aware of the Palestinian cause. It did not matter, they said, how much damage they did or how many people were killed as long as they remained a factor in any settlement in the Middle East, and terror was the only weapon left to them.

The argument raged. There was no agreement. But when the vote was taken, Arafat and his supporters proved to be the more numerous and their policy of remaining a national liberation movement was officially adopted. But it was not as simple as that. The militants, furious at being denied their terrorist activity and still bent on revenge for the death of Abu Ali Iyad, started to drift away from Fatah to join the PFLP. Fatah was in a bind. It could not sustain the loss of its young men on top of all the casualties it had taken in Jordan and southern Lebanon, but at the same time it could not agree to their plans to indulge in outright terrorism without harming its international image as the main political and military expression of Palestinian resistance.

Arafat, who carefully cultivated a Ché Guevara image with a three-day growth of beard, combat fatigues and basketball boots, was accepted as the leader of the Palestinians, a man with whom governments could negotiate, and he did not want the taint of terror to harm that image. He also did not want to embarrass the Arab governments which finance Fatah.

So it was decided to let the Revenging Palestinians have their head under the guise of a new organization which, while remaining an integral part of Fatah, could be disclaimed. It was given the name of Black September to disguise its parenthood, and its first victim, Wasfi Tell, was chosen not only because he was genuinely hated but also because he would appear to be a natural victim for a splinter group of fedayeen determined on revenge outside the control of Fatah. The Fatah leaders were therefore covered both ways: if the operation was a success their militants would be kept happy without Fatah being involved and if it was a failure Fatah would be able to discontinue Black September without losing face.

Nevertheless, the killing of Wasfi Tell was under Fatah control throughout. Abu Daoud, the Black September leader captured in Amman by the Jordanians while setting up an operation against the Jordanian government, told the Jordanians that the man who organized the killing was Mohammed Youssef el Najjar, who was known as Abu Youssef. Daoud said: "Abu Youssef personally assigned the men through Yahya Ashur, he transported them to Cairo and subsequently he himself carried their weapons to Cairo." At that time Abu Youssef was a member of the Palestine Liberation Organization's political department and chairman of the Higher Committee for Palestinian Affairs in Lebanon, a body which serves as a liaison between the 300,000 Palestinians in Lebanon and the Lebanese authorities. He was killed by the Israelis in their execution raid on Beirut on April 10, 1973.

Fatah's leadership, despite Abu Youssef's involvement in Tell's assassination, was still divided over the advisability of the use of pure terror. But the success of the assassination and the worldwide furor it caused convinced the doubters of the power of terror. The flamboyant killing of one man by a group with an evocative name had put the Palestinians back into the world's headlines. It had been more effective than a hundred dangerous missions inside Israel. Now the world had to take notice of the Palestinians. As soon as this situation became apparent, the propaganda line from Beirut made a significant switch. It had started immediately after the killing by announcing Black September's existence and claiming that the killing had been in revenge for the death of Abu Ali Iyad and Hussein's defeat of the commandos in September 1970. But then, as the world displayed its shocked interest, the line changed from revenge to the more general line of fighting for justice for the Palestinians. This switch marked the adoption by Fatah of the philosophy and practice of terror as its main weapon. Once again, the Arabs had turned to a secret society dedicated to death. Black September had not only been born, it had leaped fully armed and bloody-handed into an unsuspecting world.

2 • The Holy Cause

ARABS WHO ARE voluble about the injustices inflicted on the Palestinians and who show a considerable knowledge of the inner workings of the liberation movement grow strangely quiet when asked about Black September. They disclaim all knowledge and say, as Arafat says: "We do not know this organization and we are not involved in it but we can understand how young men will die for the life of Palestine."

They also say that Black September is more a state of mind than an actual organization. There is a great deal of truth in this, for Black September is not a clear-cut entity with full-time members and officers. It draws on Fatah members, it has arrangements with other organizations such as the PFLP to use their members for certain operations and it also recruits non-Arabs for individual missions. It has several chieftains who initiate their own operations and they can use the international structure built up, not by Black September but by Fatah, so every Fatah member could also belong to Black September. There have been instances of Fatah members being sent on missions and not being told they were Black September missions until they were under way. This duality is what made the secret of Black September so hard to break. As soon as it announced itself people started to search for an organization which did not exist and it does not exist because it is part and parcel of Fatah. But it does have a leader, and his name is Salah Khalef, known as Abu Iyad. He is no relation of Abu Ali Iyad, his names means simply Father of Iyad and is common Arab usage. Officially, he is Arafat's deputy on Fatah's command. In fact, as I was told by one of the men close to him, "he *is* Black September."

He is a schoolteacher by training, and was born in Jaffa in 1933. He is married and, wisely, keeps his wife and four children in Cairo, safe from the Israelis who are hunting him. He takes no chances, for he is Number One on their execution list, and when he is in Beirut he has the use of a dozen different apartments, sleeping in a different one every night, sometimes even getting up in the middle of the night and changing his hideout.

He was the main target for the Israelis when they sent an execution squad into Beirut on April 10, 1973, and he escaped death by chance, having first arranged to stay with one of the men who was killed, but changed his mind at the last moment. He is of medium height and sturdy build, undistinguished in a crowd and, as one man who knows him well said, "he is like a fox, he slips away at the first sniff of danger."

I met him in Cairo and he made so little an impression that when I commenced my research for the series of articles which first revealed the secrets of Black September and tried—unsuccessfully—to interview him, the friend who had originally introduced us got great pleasure out of telling me that I had already met the "man who is Black September."

He has always been a Palestinian nationalist and was one

of the first members of Fatah, but when he was teaching in Kuwait—a path followed by a number of terrorists—he was regarded as a moderate. According to Jordanian sources, his conversion to violence came after the fighting between the fedayeen and Hussein's army in 1970. He had risen to a position of some power in the Fatah hierarchy by then and so when the Jordanians moved against the fedayeen his was one of the first houses to be raided. He was captured and, according to the Jordanians, they persuaded him to address an appeal to his comrades asking them to stop fighting and to lay down their arms. The army then released him. But, say the Jordanians, he was subjected to such ridicule by the guerrillas who had fought on that he reacted by turning from moderation to the utmost violence. Like Arafat, he denies all knowledge of Black September, but he has made a number of speeches which demonstrate how close he is to the terrorists. Speaking to students in Cairo in January 1973, he defended operations undertaken in foreign countries, denying that they were terrorist in nature or were acts of desperation in a failing cause. Although they were inconsistent with the tradition of wars of liberation, he said, they were necessitated by the "condition of the Palestinian Revolution" and he emphasized that such operations "will continue on a larger scale." He also called for the setting up of more underground organizations as "the only guarantee for the perpetuation of the resistance movement . . . the plans and identity of these organizations will be a secret." Later, talking to a journalist from Beirut, he said, "When we are deprived of our elementary right to fight on our own territory in order to dislodge the usurper, it is natural that we should enlarge the field of battle. That is why we are asking all our fighters to preserve their sacred right to fight by retreating into the most complete secrecy." He has earned the fear and respect of the men and women who go out to kill and be killed in the name of Black September, and in the Fatah office in Beirut where the smart young men of the propaganda department stroll around with pistols spoiling the line of their fashionable slacks, a somewhat menacing silence falls around the visitor who asks questions about him.

As well as a leader it was also necessary to have some sort of framework on which to hang the Black September state of mind. There was one at hand: Fatah's intelligence organization, Jihaz el Razd (Reconnaissance), which Abu Iyad had once headed. Razd was ideal; it was composed not of Kalashnikov—toting wild men from the refugee camps, but of smart university graduates—many from the American University of Beirut—who could speak foreign languages, could operate in European capitals without arousing suspicion and had specialized in intelligence work. At this time Razd was the one branch of Fatah that was operating efficiently. It had set up headquarters in Rome and one of its tasks was abducting Libyan enemies of Colonel Qaddafi and shipping them home to his tender mercies. It was therefore easy to convert Razd into an instrument of terror. It had the added advantage that its people were trained in secret operations and, unlike most Arabs, they were able not to boast about their work. Abu Iyad had about fifteen men to help him. They were all top-grade. One of them, Ali Hassan Salameh, had also occupied a senior position in Razd. He has the reputation of being a bit of a dandy and a woman-chaser. But he is more than that. He is the son of Sheik Hassan Salameh, a legendary Palestinian leader who was killed fighting the Israelis in 1948. The Arabs see great symbolism in this carrying on of the fight from one generation to the next, and Salameh has acquired much prestige from his father's reputation—and an implacable desire for revenge for his death. He has also emerged as an operational leader in his own right. He was the organizer of the attack on Zaid el Rifai in London and is also believed to be responsible for the blowing up of oil tanks in Trieste, Holland and Germany. At the time of writing he is the first choice to succeed Abu Iyad as the over-all leader of Black September if the Israelis ever catch up with Abu Iyad.

One man who might have succeeded to that post is the only Black September leader so far known to have died a natural death—Fuad Shemali, a Lebanese Christian who died of cancer in Geneva in August 1972. Shemali was one of the organizers of the "Munich Massacre" of eleven members of Israel's Olympic team and he left a testament in which he called for the kidnapping and killing of people held in high esteem by the Israelis. In his lifetime he preached the sanctity of violence and when he died Black September issued a statement saying: "Black September hereby declares that the only way to compensate for his death is to implement his philosophy in its most extreme form."

Abu Youssef, who succeeded to Shemali's position, carried out his teachings to the full before he was killed by the Israelis in the raid on Beirut. He was responsible not only for the assassination of Wasfi Tell but also for the hijacking of a Sabena airliner at Lod airport in May 1972 and the capture of the Israeli Embassy in Bangkok in March 1973. His death led to the increasing involvement of Khalil al Wazir (Abu Jihad) in Black September affairs. Wazir was one of the founders of Fatah and is rated third in its leadership. He is something of a foreign affairs expert with close links with Algeria and China and is believed to have opened up Black September's liaison with the Irish Republican Army. He has been involved in two abortive operations, the attack on the Israeli Embassy in Bangkok and the Abu Daoud expedition to Amman. He is shy, lives in Damascus and is known as "the silent man."

Ghazi el Husseini, one of the relatives of the Mufti of Jerusalem who figure among the leaders of Black September, is an engineer who was educated in Germany and is the "dirty tricks" expert who supplies sophisticated equipment for specialized operations.

Another technical expert is Ahmed Afghani (Abu Motassin), who controls Fatah's finances and is deeply involved in the supply of arms and equipment to Black September.

Then there is the killer: Fakhri al Umari, head of the special services section. He was one of ten Fatah men—Abu Daoud and Ali Hassan Salameh were also among them—who were sent to Cairo on an intelligence training course in August 1968. The course lasted six weeks and covered all aspects of secret intelligence work. According to Abu Daoud's testimony, Fakhri al Umari was the "case officer" for the Munich operation and supplied the arms, eight Kalashnikovs and ten grenades, which he left in a box at the Munich railway station to be picked up by the terrorists who raided the Israeli quarters in the Olympic Village.

These men and a few others form the basis of Black September. It is an all-officer situation because the troops are readily available from the ranks of the fedayeen. When an operation is planned two or three likely candidates, men and women, are brought in from the main resistance movements, in particular Fatah and PFLP, who until recently, have worked closely together in matters of terror. Before they go into training the recruits must swear on oath their total obedience to Black September. Until they do this they will not know the nature of the operation. They are then trained for that particular operation and their squad may include foreigners and specialists. They are kept incommunicado and the utmost secrecy is involved. Often only their leader is told the full details of their assignment. This system has its disadvantages. For example, when the girl leader of the mixed Japanese-Palestinian group that hijacked a Japanese airlines Jumbo jet in July 1973 accidentally blew herself up with a grenade strapped around her waist, the surviving members of the group could not carry out the operation fully because they did not know what to do. Sometimes, likely recruits are co-opted even when there is no assignment ready for them. They are treated generously and live well, with Black September footing the bill on the assumption that when their turn comes they stand a good chance of being killed.

Abu Daoud was the first Black Septembrist to give details

of the way they work and to positively link Fatah and Arafat to Black September. He was caught by the Jordanians in February 1973 as he was driving round Amman reconnoitering government buildings for an attack by sixteen fedayeen who were to cross the border in cars with specially welded compartments laden with arms and explosives. He was dressed as a Saudi Arabian shiek and had a fifteen-year-old girl with him, posing as his wife. His objective, he said, was to "occupy the Prime Minister's office, arrest the ministers and to bargain for the release of the detainees in Jordan . . ."

He was stopped by one of the patrols that keep a tight grip on Amman, and when an examination of his passport showed him to be the father of six children while his "wife" sitting alongside him was obviously a child, the policeman became curious. Moslems are of course allowed four wives, but the situation was sufficiently intriguing for the ever-suspicious Bedouin to invite him to accompany him to the police station. Whereupon his child-bride panicked, dropped the gun and ammunition she was carrying under her robe, and they were arrested.

The tall, lean Abu Daoud sang like a bird, and the Jordanians suggest that it was because he suspected Abu Iyad had sent him on a suicide mission to get him out of the way. The reasoning behind this suspicion of double-dealing is that Abu Iyad comes from Gaza and Ibu Daoud comes from the West Bank of the Jordan and there is bitter rivalry between these two factions. When asked if it was possible that Abu Daoud was betrayed by his comrades, the Jordanians just shrug and smile. However, Abu Daoud was sufficiently convinced he had been betrayed to make it unnecessary for any of the more customary methods to be used to make him talk.

He was a big catch, one of Black September and Fatah's top leaders. He named himself as a member of the Revolutionary Council of Fatah since 1970 and he was recognized as one of Black September's chieftains in the field. The true measure of his importance is that both Black September and PFLP staged special operations to obtain his release.

The Khartoum massacre in the Saudi Arabian Embassy of the United States Ambassador, Mr. Cleo Noel, his chargé d'affaires, Mr. George Moore, and the Belgian chargé, M. Guy Eid, and the seizing of the Saudi Arabian Embassy in Paris were both carried out by terrorists who demanded his release. It is not, however, certain that Abu Daoud would have welcomed being released in this manner, for the men who carried out the Paris operation called themselves the "Punishment Group" and the idea persists that they wanted not to free Abu Daoud but to execute him for revealing Black September's secrets. In the end he was released without the help of his terrorist friends. King Hussein set him free as a result of Jordan's reconciliation with Egypt and Syria, which led to Hussein granting an amnesty for all the fedayeen he had under detention.

When Abu Daoud's confession was broadcast over Amman radio his shocked comrades accused Hussein of faking it, but this argument was destroyed when Abu Daoud, in tears, repeated what he had said on a BBC television program. It is always possible that he was lying to save his skin—he had been sentenced to death but was pardoned by Hussein—but his testimony was checked against that of the men of his group who were picked up when they crossed the Jordanian border and it tallies.

In Western intelligence circles his story is regarded as being accurate except when he talked about his own involvement with the Munich Massacre. This is a story we shall come to later.

What he had to say about the organization of Black September was particularly damaging to Fatah's claim that it has no connection with Black September.

"There is no such thing as Black September," he said. "Fatah announces its own operations under this name so that

Fatah will not appear as the direct executor of the operations. . . . Abu Iyad carries out special operations whose quality, not quantity, is accentuated. He plans for big operations like Munich. . . . In the Munich operation and the operation against the Premier's office [in Amman], it seemed to me that Abu Iyad was behind them both. Whether Abu Iyad planned with others or was working on his own I cannot say definitely. If Abu Iyad did not plan with others, the accusing finger would point at him alone." And he went on to give the first indication that Arafat might be involved with actual Black September operations by claiming that four of the men in his group were personally chosen by Arafat.

Curiously enough, Arafat began to talk almost as if he wished to be recognized as a leader of Black September soon after Abu Daoud's capture. In March 1973, when President Nimeiry of the Sudan accused the Fatah representatives in Khartoum of helping to organize the Khartoum massacre, Arafat said: "I see nothing strange in Fatah elements joining Black September. . . . Japanese, Turks, Iranians and other strugglers from foreign countries" had taken part in Black September operations, and he asked: "Is it strange therefore that Palestinians, even commandos from the various resistance groups, should join this organization?"

All this makes nonsense of Fatah's claim to know nothing about Black September. There was an Alice-in-Wonderland quality about the meeting I had with Fatah's spokesman, Abu Hatim, in his Beirut office—which at the time was under siege by the Lebanese army—and listening to him declaim passionately: "Actions undertaken by Black September have no relation with Fatah or the Palestinian Liberation Organization.

Arafat's role, however, despite his intimate knowledge of Black September and the possibility of his involvement on the fringe of operations, has been to provide the front under which the real terrorist can work. He can live in the Grand Hotels, he can talk to Presidents and generals, he can maintain the

Palestinian cause as a political entity and he can plead for that cause in the world forum. He is sustained in this position by his own character, which earns him respect in the Arab world —despite his unprepossessing appearance and his soft hand-shake. He was born in Jerusalem in 1929, writes poetry, is religious, does not drink, does not smoke and has no interest in women. He once told his sister, "I already have a wife—the Revolution." He therefore enjoys something of the reverence accorded to a holy man. Even his colloquial name, Abu Ammar—the Father of Ammar—is a typically Arab play on the name of one of the Prophet Mohammed's followers who was called Ammar ben Yasir—Ammar, the son of Yasir.

The money that finances the expensive business of terrorism comes both willingly and unwillingly from the Arab world. The "revolutionary" states of Egypt, Libya, Syria and Iraq pay annual dues to the Palestine Liberation Organization in a perfectly open fashion to support the resistance movement. Much of this money, however, is then passed to Fatah—Arafat is chairman of both organizations—and then Fatah uses it to finance the terrorist operations it carries out under the name of Black September.

In addition, the "feudal" oil-rich states of Arabia and the Gulf pay their protection money to the resistance movement. Kuwait, Saudi Arabia, Abu Dhabi and Dubai are among the states which have become the unwilling financiers of Black September outrages—a piquant situation when set alongside the avowed intention of the terrorists to destroy the feudal regimes.

Another large source is even more unwilling—the 200,000 Palestinians now working in the Gulf states and Saudi Arabia who have special taxes levied on them to help pay for the PLO. Some government officials have up to 10 percent of their salaries deducted—a tithe for terrorism. This in itself is a harking-back to an earlier terrorism; when the Mufti of Jerusalem was in Baghdad stirring up trouble for the British from 1939 to

1941, he was paid a subsidy by the Iraqi government of £1,000 a year plus 2 percent of the salaries of government employees.

But the real paymaster of terrorism is Colonel Qaddafi, who, in March 1970, said in a speech over Libyan radio that we are giving assistance to Fatah, which we consider to represent the true fedayeen action. Fatah is following a clear line." The Israelis estimate that by 1972 Qaddafi was pouring a million pounds a month into Fatah's coffers and was paying bonuses for successful operations. One report (John Laffin, *Daily Telegraph,* April 27, 1973) said that he gave Black September three million pounds as a reward for the Munich Massacre. He has also guaranteed that if Black September operations cause any of the Arab states to withdraw support, he will make up the lost money.

Other groups involved in terror have their own sources of finance. The Syrians pay for Saiqa, and the Iraqis pay for the Arab Liberation Front. The PFLP make their own money out of hijacking. In February 1972, the PFLP, which at that time was cut off from the mainstream of Fatah funds and was running short of money, hijacked a Lufthansa Jumbo jet, Flight 649 from New Delhi to Athens. The passengers, who included Joseph P. Kennedy III, the nineteen-year-old eldest son of the late Senator Robert Kennedy, had just settled down to watch the James Bond film *Diamonds Are Forever* when five Arabs brandishing pistols and grenades took over the plane, claiming to be members of the "Organization of Victims of Zionist Occupation"—one of PFLP's cover names. They forced Captain Erwin Zoller to land at Aden, where they released the passengers and demanded a straight ransom from Lufthansa: five million dollars in exchange for the plane and crew. It appears that they did not realize what a valuable property they had on board in the person of young Kennedy. However, Lufthansa succumbed to the blackmail, with West Germany's Transport Minister Georg Leber declaring that he paid the money only to save the lives of the crew—"had it been only the plane I wouldn't have given a penny." So, even though their revolutionary comrades of the People's Democratic Republic of South Yemen took a million dollars from them for "landing fees," the PFLP got away with four million dollars. They changed the notes on the Beirut money market and were back in the terrorist business. Four months later three Japanese revolutionaries belonging to the Rengo Sekigun, the "Red Army" group, were sent to Lod airport by PFLP and there they mowed down twenty-six people, mostly Puerto Rican pilgrims on a visit to the Holy Land.

Since the War of the Day of Atonement, however, it seems that the PFLP has acquired a new source of income: Colonel Qaddafi. For, although Qaddafi opposes Habash's political aims, he approves wholeheartedly of the PFLP's continued use of terror, and has allocated a supply of his oil money to PFLP to demonstrate that approval.

Arab governments also help the terrorists by providing safe bases, training and weapons. Qaddafi is once again the prime mover. As soon as Black September's existence was announced, he ordered every Libyan embassy to provide whatever help its members required. Weapons, passports, travel facilities, communications, sanctuary, everything was to be put at the terrorists' disposal in flagrant disregard of the code governing international relations.

An important role is also played by the Arab governments in justifying the terrorists' actions. After the massacre at Lod airport, the then Egyptian Prime Minister Azziz Sidki said: "This incident indicates we are capable of achieving victory in our battle against Israel." In the face of worldwide criticism he later tried to explain away this statement by saying that he was merely talking in a military sense, pointing out that the Israelis were not invincible. But he voiced no regret over the killing of innocent people who were in no way involved in the Middle East situation. The only Arab leader who has ever criticized

organized Arab terrorism in a forthright fashion is King
Hussein, the man Black September still has at the top of its
assassination list. After both Munich and Lod he was bitter in
his condemnation. Munich, he said, was an abhorrent crime
carried out by sick minds who did not belong to humanity.
Some of the other Arab leaders agreed with him in private but
they did not dare say so, not only because they have no wish
to figure on the assassination list but also because they are
forced to support any action undertaken against the Israelis
however horrific it may be. The Palestinian cause has become
holy and no Arab dare speak against it. There are also many
who believe quite passionately that their cause is so just it is
entitled to adopt any means to achieve its ends. One educated
Palestinian, a respected journalist working in Cairo, told me
that he regarded the massacre of the pilgrims at Lod by the
Japanese terrorists as "one of the most successful operations
carried out by the resistance. It was planned in order to show
that the struggle has become worldwide. It transferred the
Palestine liberation movement to the international level. Until
this operation Israel had control of the world's mass media,
but afterwards the readers and the television watchers had to
ask themselves: " 'Why was this done?' We hope that they will
find out the answer one day."

He justified the Khartoum killings by arguing that this was
one of the few ways the Palestinians could strike at the United
States, which was supplying the Israelis with the weapons used
to kill Palestinians.

In Amman, a fierce old man, onetime Mayor of Jaffa and a
political adviser to Fatah, sat sipping coffee in the afternoon
sun in his garden and justified both Lod and Khartoum in the
same fashion. "How else can we bring pressure to bear on the
world? The deaths are regrettable, but they are a fact of war
in which innocents have become involved. They are no more
innocent than the Palestinian women and children killed by the
Israelis and we are ready to carry the war all over the world.

Unless the big powers give the Palestinians back their land there will be more and more terrorism." He then used an argumen which I hear constantly as I talk to Arabs of all countries about terrorism. "Why," he asked, "should you be happy when I am unhappy? Why should the rest of the world live in comfort when the Palestinians live in refugee camps? Why should you enjoy your land while the usurpers occupy ours?"

This is the attitude that pervades the Arab countries. Its message is that everything is permissible in the fight against the Israelis and on a more fanatic level was expressed by a Voice of Palestine broadcast from Damascus on the day after Munich which said: "Glory, all glory to the men. Glory, all glory to you, men of September, glory. Glory, pride and victory as you wage the struggle in the enemy camp."

3 • The Fatal Flaw

HOW HAS IT COME about that a race which once lived by the strictest rules of chivalry and to whom honor and "face" are still of the utmost importance can now glory in the brutal murder of unarmed innocents? Part of the answer to this question lies in those aspects of Arab life I have already discussed: the tradition of secret societies which use terror for political purposes; the dreams of the golden age of the Arab empire and the reality of the present humiliation; and the deep love for the lost land of Palestine. Western apologists for the terrorists advance another reason: that the Palestinians were driven to adopt terror tactics by despair because the world had forgotten them and they could not fight against the military might of Israel except by the use of terror. All these factors are part of the answer to the question of why the Palestinians carry out acts of the most ferocious and indiscriminate murder, but they do not explain why these acts are greeted with a support which often borders on glee, not only by the terrorist organizations but also by ordinary Arabs and by Arab governments. How is it that governments that lay claim to representing civilized nations can not only support but actually finance the people who carried out the massacres at Khartoum, Lod and Athens?

The answer, I am afraid, lies in a fatal flaw in the Arab character.

After the battle of Hattin at which Saladin destroyed the power of the Crusaders, he had the three most distinguished captives—Guy and Amalric of Lusignan, who were the King and Constable of Jerusalem, and Reginald of Kerak, the Prince Arnat who had once dared to lead an expedition in an attempt to take the Holy City of Mecca—brought before him. A chronicler of the times recorded what happened: "The tent was finally put in order, and the Sultan seated himself there happily. He bade them bring in the King and his brother and the Prince Arnat. Then he offered a sherbet of chilled rose water to the King, who was overcome by thirst. He only drank a part, and offered the goblet to the Prince Arnat. The Sultan said at once to the interpreter, 'Remind the King that it is not I but he who gives drink to this man.' For the Sultan had adopted the praiseworthy and generous custom of the nomads, who granted life to a prisoner if he ate or drank of that which belonged to them.

"Then he gave order to lead the three to a place prepared for their reception, and when they had eaten, he asked for them to be brought in again. Only some servants were then with him. The King he made to sit in the vestibule; he required the Prince of Kerak to come in, and after reminding him again of the words he had spoken, he said, 'I am he who will serve Muhammad against thee!'

"He then inquired if the Prince would embrace Islam, and on the man's refusal, he drew his sword and struck him a blow which severed the arm from the shoulder. At this the servitors sprang upon the captive and God sent his soul to hell."

Haroun al Rashid, the Caliph of Baghdad of the *Thousand and One Nights,* fell passionately in love with a handsome young man, Jafar ibn Barmak, scion of one of the most powerful of Baghdad's families. He made the young man his Vizier and then in order to stop the gossip married his sister Abbassa to Jafar on condition that the marriage never was consummated. But Abbassa was a strong-willed and sensuous woman and she crept out of the harem at nights disguised as a servant to make love with her husband. She soon became pregnant and gave birth to a son but managed to conceal his existence from both her husband and her brother for some years. But then rumors reached Haroun al Rashid; he had the boy brought before him and, seeing his likeness to Jafar, had him strangled. Then it was Abbassa's turn. She was strangled by the palace eunuch. And, finally, Jafar was beheaded by the swordsman-executioner, who threw the handsome, bloodied head at the feet of the Caliph.

This happened long ago, and Prince Arnat, feared as "the Wolf of Kerak," was a brigand as well as a Crusader and no doubt deserved to die, while the Caliph's revenge can be attributed to the derangement of a betrayed lover. It can be argued that such acts were commonplace at that time among all races. It can also be argued that other, supposedly civilized, races have recently shown a savagery far surpassing anything the Arabs have done for many years. No one can dismiss the awful evidence of Hitler's concentration camps, Stalin's purges or Lieutenant Calley's massacre at My Lai. But these were aberrations inherent in the systems imposed on the people but not in the people themselves. Most of the world's peoples have developed beyond the acceptance of such violence. The Arabs, however, have remained a violent race. They are capable of blind rage, of going berserk, and while they can be as chivalrous as Saladin and as illustrious as Haroun al Rashid, they can also be as savage as the former and as cruel at the latter.

They also have the unfortunate habit of choosing as their leaders zealots from the fringes of sanity who can whip mobs into frenzy by the power of their oratory and then set them loose to burn and kill.

The Koran forbids the portrayal of the human face and figure and this restriction on Moslem artists has led first to the development of intricate geometric patterns and secondly to the development of speech as an artistic form. Words are embellished, phrases polished and elaborated, complicated puns are woven into the fabric of a speech until the sheer beauty of the words becomes more important than the message of the speech. When the aged woman singer Oum Kalthoum gives one of her concerts, the whole of the Arab world comes to a halt. Tickets to these concerts cost up to five hundred dollars and throughout the Middle East men crowd in ecstasy around their radios listening to her elaborate on one phrase sometimes for fifteen or twenty minutes at a time. Her songs last for hours and she has command of an audience of millions. Given this power of the word, it takes little to whip a mob into a killing frenzy. When King Faisal of Iraq was overthrown in 1958, the royal family was murdered and Nuri Said, the strong man of the government, was caught by such a mob and literally torn to pieces. Sometimes it is not even necessary to use words to touch the fatal flaw; emotion alone will do it. When Nasser died, the Egyptians were so crazed with grief that literally millions of people poured onto the streets of Cairo and tore their leader's coffin from its gun carriage and passed it from hand to hand to his tomb.

The atmosphere in Cairo was so charged with emotion that night that the authorities feared a repetition of Black Saturday, January 26, 1952, when an officially encouraged mob set fire to British establishments in the city but then got out of hand when Moslem Brotherhood agitators urged them on to burn and loot until the whole of the city was in danger of being put to the torch.

The undercurrent of violence is present in everyday Arab

life—nobody who has experienced the traffic in Beirut, where ordinary traffic arguments often end in shoot-outs, will doubt this statement—and the fatal flaw is compounded by the fatalism taught in the Koran: everything is written and nothing can be undone, but believers who fall in battle will go straight to Paradise. It is a continuing tradition of the Arabs to cut off the genitals of their dead enemies—and this happened to the Israeli defenders of Mount Harmon during the War of the Day of Atonement—in order not only to degrade their manhood and frighten their comrades but also to make sure they do not enjoy the sexual pleasures of Paradise.

Most of the more extreme terrorists are Marxists or revolutionaries from even farther to the left who do not believe in religion and are committed to building their Paradise on earth. But even they cannot ignore the effect of the clash of religions in the present conflict. How can they when in Jerusalem, the focal point of the conflict, the Aqsa mosque, one of the holiest places of Islam, stands upon the site of Herod's temple, the physical center of Judaism?

Alongside Aqsa there is the magnificent golden Dome of the Rock, built over the spot to which, in Mohammed's vision, he was carried from Mecca one night on his legendary horse al-Burak, and from there was carried up through the seven heavens into the presence of Allah. This very same rock is also believed to have been the improvised altar on which Abraham prepared to sacrifice his son Isaac, as well as being the site of the Holy of Holies of the Jewish temple.

There can be little surprise, then, at the Arabs' desire to regain control of Jerusalem and their lost holy places, just as the Jews for two thousand years vowed at each Passover: "Next year in Jerusalem." In this the Arabs of the far left are at one with King Faisal, the feudal monarch who regards himself as the custodian of Islam.

Five years ago the editor-in-chief of the Jordanian newspaper *Al Massa* wrote: "When we consider the history of

Jerusalem, we shall learn that seventy thousand fighters fell on its walls until it was liberated, saved and made Arabic. The blood of all these will pour curses on Arabs and Moslems alike should a single grain of Jerusalem's holy earth be lost.

"In history, the conquest of Jerusalem knew only one language, the language of honor, glory and faith, of violence, victims and blood. If the Arabs want to save Jerusalem today from Zionist pollution and deceit, they will only succeed by kindling a popular war of Arabs and Moslems. Israel, which sees the conquest of Jerusalem as the realization of the dreams of generations, will not give up our holiest place. They will do so only as the Crusaders did, by being annihilated, even at the price of another seventy thousand victims."

Here, then, we have the fabric of terrorism. It is woven from zealotry, humiliation, history, despair, love for the lost land and the fatal flaw of inherent violence, and it is patterned by a hatred which, while being directed at the Israelis, has become almost casual in its application. George Habash spelled out his lack of concern for the innocents involved in his acts of terrorism as long ago as 1969, when, after his men blew up an oil pipeline, he was asked by Lee Grigg of *Time* magazine: "Does not the blowing up of the pipeline, which you have said is aimed at American interests, also hurt Arab interests at the same time?" Habash replied: "It may, but that is no concern of ours. There are many Arab millionaires made rich by oil or by representing Western companies. It is not right that they should be rich while we are both poor and homeless. They are indirectly the agents of the United States, which aids Israel. I know blowing up the Tapline hurts Saudi Arabia. But Saudi Arabia is a reactionary regime, and it sells its oil to those who support Israel. It is too bad for Saudi Arabia that she may suffer. Our main aim remains American interests."

Grigg then asked: "Does Israeli retaliation for your raids, which often kills innocent Arab civilians bother you?" And Habash answered: "No. It is exactly what we want, for we are totally against any peaceful solution that leaves behind an Israel. And this is the only possible peaceful solution in prospect."

The interview continued. Grigg: "Will there be other 'spectaculars'?" Habash: "Yes, there must be. We must mobilize our people, and to do so we must continue our present policies. What we are after is the liberation of Palestine. If we must blow up a dozen El Al planes to do it, then we will. Liberation is only accomplished by consistent and insistent popular war."

Grigg: "Does it matter to you that the Middle East crisis might develop into a World War?" Habash: "Not really. The world has forgotten Palestine. Now it must pay attention to our struggle."

At the same time Yasir Arafat was telling a Moroccan journalist: "The objective of our war at this stage of the struggle is to do away with the social, economic and political fortress of Israel in a long and protracted war which must of necessity end in success. The Tartars ruled this country for seventy years and the Crusaders for nearly two hundred years; but in the end they were defeated and nothing was left of them."

There is a subtle difference in the language of Habash and Arafat which was later to reflect the difference in operations carried out by the Fatah-controlled Black September and the PFLP terrorists. The Black September operations have always been aimed at carefully selected people or establishments whose destruction could—by terrorist standards—be classed as an act of war against the Israelis. But PFLP's operations have, more often than not, been of an indiscriminate nature involving the slaughter of innocents in no way connected with the struggle between the Israelis and the Palestinians.

However, there is no doubt about the principal aim of the rival groups of terrorists. It is the destruction of the State of Israel. The Fatah monthly publication, *The Palestinian Revolution*, while explaining why a conventional war does not suit the Palestinian goal, in its issue of June 1968 said: "For the aim of this war is not to impose our will on the enemy but to destroy him in order to take his place. . . . In a conventional war there is no need to continue the war if the enemy submits to our will . . . while in a people's war there is no deterrent, for its aim is not to subjugate the enemy but to destroy him. A conventional war has limited aims which cannot be transcended, for it is necessary to allow the enemy to exist in order to impose our will over him, while in a people's war destruction of the enemy is the first and last duty." It is significant that the Arab expression *ifna* was used for "destroy" in this passage, for its literal meaning is "reduction to absolute nothingness."

It is statements like this that set the truth free, for it is certain that the Arabs do want to reduce Israel to "absolute nothingness." However, for diplomatic reasons they have been forced to moderate their language and for the past few years they have been talking about the replacing of the "Zionist-Imperialist State of Israel" with a "truly democratic Palestine" in which Arab and Jew and Christian can live together in harmony. Fatah told the United Nations that its objectives are: (1) the liberation of the whole of Palestine from foreign occupation and aggression and (2) the formation of an independent, democratic, sovereign Palestinian state, where all legitimate and legal inhabitants share equal rights, irrespective of religion or language.

But this would entail the destruction of Israel as we know it, for under the Arab plan the number of Jews who would be allowed to live in this new Palestine would be limited to those who lived in Palestine before 1917 and their offspring. The rest, including all those who fled from the remains of Hitler's Europe, would have to return to their country of origin.

It is nonsense of course, and now, in the wake of the October War, Arafat and his followers are pursuing a more pragmatic course, hoping to see the establishment of an Arab Palestinian state in either Gaza or on the West Bank of the Jordan.

But for the extremists the setting up of such a state would be an Israeli trick designed to confirm Israel's occupation of the heartland of Palestine. They have coined several derogatory names for it calling it "Al-Kian al-hazil" (the emaciated entity) and Duwaila (the mini-state). And, despite the efforts of those moderates who have had enough bloodshed and would settle for their mini-state, the hard men have no intention of living in coexistence with Israel. Their objective remains the destruction of the State of Israel and, for George Habash and his Marxist followers, it is allied to the overthrow of the Arab sheikdoms and the dream of world revolution. It is in these men that the fatal flaw runs wide and deep. These are the men who glory in the slaughter of innocents not only because they see indiscriminate terror as the way to achieve their ambitions but also because violence lurks like some evil djinn in their souls.

4 • The Killing at Lod

THE PERIOD IMMEDIATELY after the killing of Wasfi Tell and the attempt on Zaid el Rifai was a quiet one as Fatah capitalized on the Revenging Palestinians' success and planned a full-scale campaign of terror. Minor operations were carried out against factories in Germany and gas installations in Holland. On February 6, 1972, oil tanks belonging to Gulf Oil were set on fire in Holland and on the same day five Jordanians were murdered in West Germany after they had been accused of collaborating with the Israelis. Two days later the Streuber Motor factory, which was making engines for Israel in Hamburg, was blown up and on February 22 the Esso Oil pipeline near Hamburg was damaged. Black September claimed responsibility for these operations and accused the companies involved of helping the Israelis.

Then, on May 8, Black September got into the hijacking

business. Sabena Flight 517 from Brussels to Tel Aviv was over Zagreb when two men and two girls performed the by now customary act of waving pistols and grenades and taking over the plane. But their plan was more audacious than usual. They ordered the captain, Reginald Levy, a British Jew, to fly his Boeing 707 on to Lod airport, his original destination. The plan was to show that the Israelis were open to attack on their own territory by threatening to blow up the plane, its 87 passengers and 10 crew members if the Israelis did not release 319 imprisoned fedayeen. Captain Levy, whose wife was aboard the plane, radioed ahead to Lod and told the control tower what was happening. General Moshe Dayan, the Defense Minister, was immediately informed and he hurried to the airport with a picked team of paratroopers to meet the plane. As soon as it rolled to a halt in the warm dusk, soldiers disguised as mechanics let down the tires and drained the hydraulic system. Meanwhile, the hijackers had contacted the control tower and made their demands. The Israelis started to negotiate, but, said the Chief of Staff, General David Elazar, later, "We never proposed to hand over any prisoners to them. All our negotiations were playing for time until the right moment."

The Israelis also allowed representatives of the Red Cross to negotiate with the terrorists and later the Red Cross was to complain that its officials had been deceived by the Israelis. The negotiations dragged on for twenty hours and at one point, said Captain Levy, he was sure that they were all about to be blown up. "The Arabs were getting very agitated because the Israelis would not hand over the fedayeen. The two girls had already mined the plane with plastic charges. They were all carrying grenades and they decided to blow us all to Kingdom Come, themselves included. When I saw the girls crying and kissing the two men goodbye before they let off the charges I knew something had to be done. I grabbed one man's gun. I squeezed the trigger. It didn't go off. The safety catch was on. Don't ask me why, but they didn't shoot us. And we managed to talk them into delaying the blowing-up operation."

Meanwhile, Dayan's team of paratroopers had been practicing assault tactics on another Boeing 707. When they were able to force the doors, climb inside and start shooting in ninety seconds, General Elazar decided that the right moment had come. The paratroopers, dressed in technicians' white overalls, walked to the airliner as if they were going to carry out repairs. Then they attacked. "It all happened at once," said one passenger. "Suddenly the doors were torn open and the Israelis were in the plane firing everywhere and shouting, 'Lie down, lie down, it's all over!' " Another passenger decribed the scene like this: "Suddenly the escape hatch opened and a man in white jumped in and shot one Arab right between the eyes. Then all the hatches opened. There was a lot of shooting."

It lasted ten seconds. At the end of that time the Palestinian men, who were named by Black September as Major Ahmed Mousa Awad and Lieutenant Abdel Aziz el Atrash, lay dead, while their girl companions were captured. One of them, Therese Halsa, was wounded, while the other, Rima Tannous, who had had been armed with a grenade, was thrown to the floor by one of the paratroopers. Several passengers were injured and one of them, twenty-two-year-old Mrs. Miriam Anderson, died later in a hospital. For Captain Levy, who won the DFC as an RAF bomber pilot, it was a memorable fiftieth birthday.

The trial of the two girl hijackers, held before a military court in the cinema of the old British army camp at Sarafand, provided some interesting details about the way Black September operates. The two girls displayed completely different characters. Nineteen-year-old Therese showed that she was a typical example of a committed terrorist. Born near Nazareth, daughter of a middle-class Arab family living under Israeli rule, she completed high school and became a nursing student. Like so many Arabs of her generation, she had had hatred of the Israelis drummed into her. She was recruited into Fatah by a fellow student and in 1971 she made her way across the border to report to a Fatah base for duty. She took to terrorism willingly and happily.

Twenty-one-year-old Rima told a different story. An orphan, not overly endowed with intelligence, she was brought up by nuns and drifted into nursing in Amman. She gave a harrowing account of being raped by a young man and then becoming the mistress of a doctor who introduced her to drugs and to Fatah. Once recruited, she said, she was forced to sleep with Fatah members, being beaten or deprived of the morphine to which she had become addicted if she refused. She became totally dependent on Fatah for food rations and the small salary it pays its members. Weeping, she told the Israeli court: "I had to comply with their orders. I had as much free will as a robot."

Before her trial Therese told General Rehaven Zeevi, commander of Israel's Central District, which includes Lod airport, that before the operation, "we spent three days in Brussels shopping, dining at expensive restaurants and dancing in the evenings." They also shared bedrooms with their male colleagues but she swore that "nothing happened."

In her confession Therese told how she was selected for special operations, subjected to an intense test of loyalty and then trained in sabotage. Eventually she and Rima were sent on their mission. They knew the two men with them as Yosef and Zechariah. They knew that the linen body belts they had been given contained plastic explosives and that their handbags and cans of talcum powder concealed grenades and pistols.

What they did not know, she said, was the precise target for their mission. Only after the Boeing had taken off from Vienna on the second leg of its flight to Tel Aviv did they realize they were bound for Israel, although they had boarded the plane carrying forged Israeli passports and speaking pidgin Hebrew.

They were found guilty on three charges brought under the British emergency regulations of 1945, which are still in force in Israel: membership in a group which committed offenses involving the use of weapons and explosives; carrying weapons, ammunition, grenades and explosives; and membership in an illegal organization, Fatah. One of the three judges demanded the death sentence: "They were both nurses," he argued, "angels who should have saved people's lives. Instead they brought death to innocent people. Life imprisonment should be insufficient for them and the death sentence would serve as a deterrent."

He was overruled, and the two girls were sentenced to life imprisonment. As they were led away they both made remarks which again reflected their different characters. Therese said: "I knew it would end like this. But it is too severe. I shall be an old woman when I get out." And Rima, weeping said: "My life in an Israeli jail is far better than the life I had before."

Rima's story demonstrated the ruthlessness with which Black September is prepared to use people, and the way in which Moshe Dayan's men stormed the airliner demonstrated the ruthlessness with which the Israelis are determined to resist Black September. The Israelis insist that any submission to blackmail will merely entail greater suffering in the future and they are prepared to spend lives to make sure that they never do submit to blackmail.

The Sabena affair was a bad defeat for Black September, a defeat that would have to be wiped out in convincing fashion if the organization was going to maintain credibility. The foundation for that revenge was laid that same month when George Habash of the PFLP convened a secret meeting of international terrorists at the PFLP-controlled Baddawi refugee camp just outside Tripoli in Lebanon.

This extraordinary affair was an attempt to pool the violence, the cunning and the fanaticism of revolutionaries from all over the world, irrespective of their political shading, in the common cause of helping each other destroy what they did not like about the world. The PFLP issued invitations only to those organizations which had distinguished themselves by their fanaticism in their own national spheres. They included emissaries from the IRA, from the Baader-Meinhof anarchist gang of West

Germany, from the Japanese "Red Army," from the "Liberation Front" of Iran and from the Turkish "People's Liberation Army." Black September sent two representatives: Abu Iyad and Fuad Shemali. Khalil al Wazir attended on behalf of Fatah. The most elaborate precautions were taken to get the foreign representatives safely into Lebanon and then home again. Many were provided with false passports, forged especially for this journey, and produced on the delegates' behalf by Libyan, Iraqi and South Yemeni embassies. Habash and his guests must have felt that all the trouble was worthwhile, however, for this polyglot assembly, linked only by their hatred for the established order and their belief in violence as a legitimate weapon, reached unanimity. They agreed on an elaborate and universal exchange attack system. Under this agreement the various organizations pledged themselves not only to assist any of the other groups but also to carry out attacks on their behalf. This meant, for example, that a Turkish target nominated by the Iranians could be dealt with by the Turkish "People's Liberation Army" or that a German target named by the Palestinians could be tackled by Baader-Meinhof.

By this time Black September and PFLP were working closely together in an alliance forged by Abu Iyad and Wadi Haddad, and on May 30, 1972, PFLP carried out an operation that not only avenged Black September for the defeat at Lod airport but also demonstrated George Habash's policy of international terrorism at work.

It was a spectacularly horrifying piece of work. Three young Japanese who had arrived at Lod airport on board Air France Flight 132 from Paris and Rome collected their fiberglass suitcases from the conveyor belt in the long, high-ceilinged arrival lounge, took off their jackets and bent down to open their cases. When they straightened up they were holding Czech-made VZT-58 automatic rifles from which the butts had been removed and half a dozen powerful shrapnel grenades. They gave no warning but started to fire into the people grouped around the conveyor belt. Then they threw their grenades. Within a minute destroyed bodies littered the hall. Blood, baggage and fragments of flesh covered the floor as twenty-four people died and seventy-eight fell wounded. Two of the attackers were also dead, one of them cut down accidentally by bullets from one of his wildly firing companions and the other decapitated by one of his own grenades. Among the dead was Professor Aharon Katchalsky, one of the world's leading scientists, an authority on biophysics. Many of the others were Puerto Rican pilgrims on a package tour of the Holy Land. One of the survivors was later quoted as saying: "How does it happen that Japanese kill Puerto Ricans because Arabs hate Israelis?"

That was the question that the Israelis wanted to ask the one surviving Japanese, who was captured by Hannan Claude Zeiton, an El Al traffic officer. Zeiton tackled the Japanese when he ran onto the tarmac outside the terminal in an attempt to blow up one of the planes parked there after he had emptied his rifle into the people in the departure lounge. "I saw him throw two grenades," said Zeiton, "I ran after him and caught him around the neck. I held him until reinforcements came."

He turned out to be an extraordinary capture, for, although he claimed to be Daisuke Namba, as his passport described him, that name belonged to another notorious Japanese, one who was executed for the attempted assassination of the then Crown Prince Hirohito in 1923. His real name was Kozo Okamoto. The passports of all three men were of ritual significance. Okamoto's gave his birthdate as December 7, the day of Japan's attack on Pearl Harbor. Jiro Sugisaki, whose real name was Takeshi Okidoro, and who blew off his own head, had his birthdate shown as February 26, the day in 1937 when officers of the Japanese army took part in an uprising. The other dead man, who gave his name as Ken Torio, was in fact Yasuiki Yashuda and he chose March 30 for his birthdate—the date of the first hijacking of a Japanese airliner when Okamoto's brother was one of a group of Red Army members who forced the pilot to fly to North Korea. The name of the mission had significance too; it was named after Patrick Arguello, the terrorist killed in the Leila Khaled hijack. The three men also carried tiny paper dolls as lucky charms. When the police first searched Okamoto they found his doll. Then, in the bloody confusion of the arrival lounge, when the police were going through the pockets of the dead and found a similar doll on the body of the man without a head, they knew they had found another of the attackers.

Gradually the story was pieced together. Yashuki Tsukuda, director of the Aliens Office of the Japanese National Police Agency, flew to Tel Aviv to help the Israeli authorities, and in a typically Japanese gesture the government sent a special envoy, Kenji Fukunaga, to apologize to the Israelis. Okamoto at first refused to talk, saying that he had completed his mission and now all he wanted to do was to be allowed to commit suicide. General Zeevi, the man who interrogated Therese Halsa and Rima Tannous after the Sabena affair, threw a pistol on the table in front of him and told him he could use it on himself if he would sign an already written confession. Okamoto broke down and signed, and talked.

He and his comrades, he said, were members of the Rengo Sekigun, the Red Army. This is a particularly vicious little organization spawned by the Japanese protest movement. It has a kamikaze-type philosophy and its leaders had purged by torture and murder at least a dozen of its members, including one pregnant girl who was thought to be "too bourgeois." Most of its members were in fact from bourgeois families and were university dropouts. Okamoto had been an agricultural student at Kagoshima University. The connection with the PFLP started early in 1970 when an Iraqi revolutionary, code named Bassim, who later married Leila Khaled, visited Tokyo, thus following in his leader, George Habash's footsteps to the East. (Habash sees North Korea as the perfect revolutionary country and would like to become Palestine's Kim Il Sung.) Bassim contacted the Red Army and the two organizations made a film together called *Revolutionary War Declared*. In November 1971, Okamoto was asked to arrange a showing of this film at his university, and later he was invited to go to Beirut, where his brother was already undergoing training with the PFLP.

"I received a letter requesting me to leave for Tokyo at the end of February or the beginning of March, and to go from there to Montreal, New York and Paris. From New York I was supposed to fly by El Al 747 first-class, to observe everything closely and remember every detail and when I reached Beirut to make contact with a certain Japanese who would make all the arrangements for me. . . .

"After arriving in Beirut, I went by taxi to Baalbek. In the house where I arrived, we stayed all three of us, Okidoro, Yasuda and I. We did gymnastics to get fit and afterward we trained in Port Said, in explosives, shooting with pistols and Kalashnikovs, and hand grenades. On May 16, I was told by Okidoro that four Japanese would take part in a military operation, and from May 17 we went through training for this military operation."

They left Beirut for Paris on May 22 and arrived in Rome on May 30, where they booked into the Anglo-American Hotel for a night before moving to the Scaligera Pension in the Via Nazionale, where Arabs often stay. On May 30 they checked in at Leonardo da Vinci airport for the flight to Tel Aviv. They passed through the body search at the airport, which made sure that they were not carrying any weapons onto the aircraft. But their baggage was not opened or checked in any way—a loophole in security which was to cost twenty-six lives and cause a furious three-way row, with Israel accusing the French of neglecting to mount proper safeguards and the French saying it was the responsibility of the Italians. Whoever was to blame, the fact remained that three Japanese massacred a number of people, mainly Puerto Ricans in Israel, on behalf of the Palestinians. Why?

Okamoto answered that question at his trial in a bizarre speech delivered, poker-faced, to a court which could hardly believe what it heard.

He and his companions, he said, had decided that their revolutionary operation had to be carried out decisively. "This was our duty, to the people I slaughtered and to my two comrades who lost their lives. It is my response with the other soldiers, to the people I killed. I take on myself full responsibility for it. . . .

"The revolutionary struggle is a political struggle between the classes. It is a just struggle. We strive to build a world where wars will be banished. But it will be a long struggle and we are preparing World War Three through our own war, through killing people, destroying houses, annihilating property. . . .

"War involves slaughtering and destruction. We cannot limit warfare to destruction of buildings. We believe slaughtering of human bodies is inevitable. We know it will become more severe than battles between nations. . . .

"This incident has been reported worldwide, but it seems to me nobody has grasped the motivation for it. But when a similar operation takes place the next time what will the world think? When I was captured, a certain Japanese asked me: 'Was there no other way?' Can that man propose an alternative method?

"I believe that, as a means toward world revolution, I must prepare the creation of the world Red Army."

The decision by the Red Army to enter into a relationship with the PFLP was, he said, "a means of propelling ourselves onto the world stage. . . . The Arab world lacks spiritual fervor, so we felt that through this attempt we could stir up the Arab world. The present world order has given Israel power which has been denied the Arab refugees. This is the link between the Japanese Red Army and the Popular Front for the Liberation of Palestine, with whom we collaborate. . . .

"I want you to know that the next target may be New York or San Francisco. I would like to warn the entire world that we will slay anyone who stands on the side of the bourgeoisie. This I do not say as a joke." It is hardly necessary to point out that nobody in the court was laughing during this extraordinary performance.

He ended his speech by saying: "We three soldiers, after we die, want to become three stars of Orion. When we were young we were told that if we died we may become stars in the sky. I may not have fully believed it but I was ready to. I believe some of those we slaughtered have become stars in the sky. The revolution will go on and there will be many more stars. But if we recognize that we go to the same heaven, we can have peace."

He was sentenced to life imprisonment, with the presiding judge Lieutenant Colonel Abraham Frisch, saying that he deserved to be hanged but that the court felt it would not be right to go beyond what the prosecutor had asked, "even if we believe justice demands it."

Addressing Okamoto, the judge said: "It is worthwhile that you know what your image is. . . . You come under the mask of a guest with intentions of murder. Many of your victims were guests from a far-off country. You spilled innocent blood. This is your image. You have taken yourself outside the pale of any human society. There is no penalty commensurate to the magnitude of your crime."

But that was not how Okamoto was regarded by the PFLP, from which, out of its headquarters on the Corniche el Mazra, just a stone's throw from Beirut's fashionable beach, came a flow of announcements extolling the Japanese as fighters for justice and justifying the slaughter: "The mere choice of our occupied territory as a place for tourism is in itself a bias in favor of the enemy."

The PFLP has its origins in a movement called Quamiyin al Arab, which was founded by George Habash in 1959 with the financial and operational support of the Egyptian government and which carried out subversive activities against Jordan, Lebanon, Saudi Arabia and Kuwait on behalf of the Egyptians. Eight years later three organizations which had connections with Quamiyin decided to unite and call itself the Popular Front for the Liberation of Palestine. Since that time it has become more and more of a secret society and more and more extreme in its Marxist-Maoist attitudes. It has also spawned its own offshoots which are even more extreme. One, as noted earlier, is the Popular Democratic Front for the Liberation of Palestine led by Naif Hawatmeh, once Habash's best friend and chief lieutenant but who now claims he is the only true Marxist-Leninist in the Palestinian movement. Another, smaller group is the PFLP–General Command under the leadership of Ahmed Jibril. This group split away in 1968 because it did not approve of involving innocent people in acts of terrorism. But since then it has swung around full circle to embrace terrorism.

George Habash fell ill with heart trouble in 1972 and the operational side of PFLP has been taken over by Wadi Haddad, a doctor like Habash. Haddad lived in a flat in Beirut which was attacked with rockets fired from an apartment across the street. He was unhurt but very much shaken and now stays in hiding. It is he whom the Israelis believe responsible for the Lod massacre and therefore he has every reason to stay under cover. The front man is Bassam Abu Sherif, editor of PFLP's newspaper, *Al Hadaf*. And he is a living symbol of the viciousness of the war between the fedayeen and the Israelis. His face is mutilated, he is blind in one eye, and both hands are mangled —the effects of an Israeli letter bomb. He is also one of the men whom Okamoto met in Beirut. His office is cluttered with the paraphernalia of revolution, tail fins of rockets, spent cartridge cases, Ché Guevara posters, Kim Il Sung's books, the coats-of-arms torn from the walls of the American and Jordanian embassies and a poster showing a Viet Cong handing over a banner bearing the slogan "Victory" to a Palestinian.

There are also the pictures of various left-wing folk heroes: Lenin and Mao, James Connolly and Wolfe Tone. Connolly is quoted: "The Socialist of another country is a fellow patriot, as the capitalist of our own country is a natural enemy."

It is all rather theatrical, the sort of place Hollywood would design as a typical revolutionary's office, and it seems unreal until one hears Abu Sherif talk. He sips cups of sweet Arab coffee and speaks in a most rational fashion. It is only when one listens to the meaning of his quiet words that one realizes his mind is as scarred as his face.

He makes no bones about PFLP's objective. It is world revolution: "We are a Marxist-Leninist organization which does not see the liberation of Palestine as the ultimate aim. Politically speaking, we form an important cadre of organic rapport between the Palestinian and international revolutions. We are allied with the world progressive movement in general, I would rather ally myself to the Japanese who has been exploited than to the rich Palestinian who exploits. This is a class struggle. The poor people are realizing they are being exploited. The Jews too. We do not fight Jews. In fact, we regard the exploited and the progressive Jews as our allies in the struggle against Zionism and imperialism."

What about the use of Japanese fanatics to carry out acts of terror? "They were exploited people. They were fighting against the imperialists who exploit them." What about the killing of innocent people at Lod? (He called it Lydda, the Arab name.) He argued that the innocents should not have been there, he repeated the line that "the choice of our occupied territory as a place for tourism is in itself a bias in favor of the enemy," and he insisted, "we intend to attack imperialist and Zionist interests wherever we find them in the world. They are legal targets."

PFLP turns this philosophy into murderous reality and has provided a pattern for Black September which now uses the PFLP's method of individual cells and cut-offs to maintain security. The two organizations also reached an operational agreement. In one hijacking, PFLP cell members working at Damascus airport were able to hide guns in the seats of a Lufthansa airliner for Black September hijackers.

After Lod, the terrorists were riding high. Despite the condemnation of the massacre in the Western world, PFLP and Black September felt that they had at last achieved one of their aims, to make the rest of the world take notice of the Palestinians, and they followed up Lod with two operations, one a success and the other a failure.

The success came on August 5, 1972, when Black September blew up the trans-Alpine oil terminal at Trieste, destroying millions of gallons of oil in a fire that burned for two days at the internationally owned terminal. A gang consisting of Arabs, an Italian and two Frenchmen is credited with bringing off this coup. The failure came eleven days later when a plot to blow up an El Al Boeing 707 in mid-air on its way from Rome to Lod narrowly failed. It started when two Palestinians in Rome, Adnam Ali Hasham and Ahmed Zaid, a student leader, picked up two English girls on holiday in Italy. The girls fell for the handsome Palestinians, who suggested they should all go to Israel. The girls agreed and the Arabs bought them tickets to Lod and gave them a gift, a tape recorder. At the last moment the two men, who were posing as Iranians, said they had to fly to Teheran to collect money. They arranged to meet in Jerusalem. The girls, luckily, did not carry the tape recorder as hand baggage, but had it put in the hold with their other luggage, for inside the tape recorder was a bomb with a barometric firing device designed to explode the bomb when the jet reached a certain altitude. It exploded precisely as it was designed to do, but the force of the explosion was contained by the armored hold, constructed in all El Al planes after tests with explosions in mid-air over the desert. The damaged plane landed safely, and when the two girls had told their story, Hasham and Zaid were arrested. However, they were very soon given "provisional liberty" on the grounds that the explosive charge they used "was not adequate to destroy the airliner." Naturally, they disappeared from Italy as soon as the prison gates opened. This was one of the more flagrant examples of European countries trying to wash their hands of the whole nasty terrorist business. This operation has been credited to the PFLP–General Command. But the next one was purely Black September. And it was to be the most spectacular act of terror the world has yet seen: the massacre at the Munich Olympics.

5 • The Massacre at Munich

Munich is likely to prove to be Black September's own Karameh, its greatest success which at the same time sowed the seeds of its own destruction. The success, in the terrorist terms of forcing the world to take notice of the Palestinians, could not be bettered. Television, geared to show the games to every corner of the globe by satellite, gave the world a front-row seat to watch the day-long drama which left eleven members of the Israeli team, five Black Septembrists and one German policeman dead after the battle at Fürstenfeldbruck airfield. Millions of people agonized over the harrowing pictures of terrorism at work in a setting designed to emphasize brotherhood of man and the joy of peaceful competition. But while so many saw the denouement of the plot, few knew the details of its organization and none could know what results it would have.

One of the few men who knew about the plot was Abu Daoud. The story he told his Jordanian interrogators was that he was in Sofia buying arms for Fatah at the beginning of August 1972 and traveling with a forged Iraqi passport under the name of Saad ad-Din Wali when Abu Iyad arrived from Geneva with Fakhri al Umari and told him about the plan to attack the Israeli team at the Olympic Games.

According to Abu Daoud, the Black September leader asked him to give his Iraqi passport to Fakhri al Umari because it contained a valid German visa. Abu Daoud maintains that he did this after he had returned from Libya and swears that he took no further part in the operation but was later told by Abu Iyad and Fakhri al Umari what had happened. However, Western intelligence services are convinced that Abu Daoud used the Iraqi passport himself, was present throughout the operation and was one of its principal organizers. German police investigators discovered that Fakhri al Umari and a man who called himself Saad ad-Din Wali were in Munich at the same time and they are certain that Saad ad-Din Wali, whose Iraqi passport gave his occupation as journalism, was Abu Daoud. The records show that he was registered at a small Munich hotel from late June until September 5, the day of the massacre. The Western authorities believe that he hid his connection with the Munich affair—and that the Jordanian authorities allowed him to do so—to avoid any international demand for his extradition and trial. It also explains why such strenuous efforts were made to secure his release. However, while Abu Daoud's claim that he was not involved is not believed, the rest of his story is, and it caused the most extreme embarrassment to Yasir Arafat and Abu Iyad. This is his account of Munich as it was broadcast over Amman radio:

"Three days after my return to Libya, Abu Iyad contacted Fakhri al Umari and asked him to go to Munich with Yusuf Nazzal, who was traveling on an Algerian passport. In Munich, Fakhri al Umari tried to enter and reconnoiter the Olympic

Village but he was turned away. He was obliged to get another person to help him. He got Mohammed Masalhah from Libya because he knows several languages, including German, and had worked as an architect in the Olympic Village while it was being built.

"It was Masalhah who reconnoitered the Village, using his cleverness, his good German and his knowledge of the entrances. He was able to learn where the Israelis were staying, which was opposite the Saudi team. The Saudis did not know anything about this operation, but Masalhah got into their quarters in his capacity as an architect and he was able to find out that the Israeli building was similar to the Saudi building and so plan the attack.

"Masalhah had taken with him the instructions for the operation from Abu Iyad. He had a statement written in English and a list of the fedayeen detainees whose release was to be demanded. Two groups totaling six were to take part in the operation, making eight with Masalhah and Yusuf Nazzal. They were to detain the Israeli team and negotiate for the release of the fedayeen. The code name for the operation was Ikrit and Birim [the names of two Arab villages which the Israelis occupied in 1948 and have refused to give back]. If the Israelis released their prisoners and took them to any Arab country except Lebanon or Jordan, the members of the Israeli team were to be taken with the eight men by plane to Tunisia and there they would have been released. In the event of a refusal, they were to go in a plane to Tunis, provided they were able to safeguard their travel to the airport in a closed van. The instructions did not include opening fire on the Israeli team. . . .

"The youths had come from Libya. Some of them came via Rome to Munich and the others came via Belgrade. Each group was composed of three people. The first group arrived on September 2 and the second the following day. Fakhri al Umari supplied the arms in two installments, the first on September 1 and the second on the morning of September 4. The arms consisted of eight Kalashnikovs and ten grenades. Mohammed

Masalhah took the arms from a box at the railway station, where they had been left by Fakhri al Umari. Mohammed Masalhah and Yusuf Nazzal booked the youths into hotels in Munich.

"Fakhri al Umari left on September 4 for Rome before the operation started and from there he went to Tripoli in Libya. After one day he flew to Beirut and then went to Damascus, where he remained. . . .

"The man responsible for the Munich operation was the acting political officer Mohammed Masalhah. No German nationals or Arabs resident in Germany took part in the operation. . . . The plan was that the young men would jump over the wall at 0400 on September 5."

This they did. Two guards saw them, but as they were dressed in track suits and carried large bags the guards assumed they were athletes who had been out late and were returning home in an unconventional fashion. They made directly for the Israeli quarters, burst in and killed two men who tried to tackle them, Joseph Romano, a weightlifter, and Moshe Weinberg, the wrestling coach. They seized nine other sportsmen and officials as hostages and then presented their demands. The negotiations went on most of the day, deadline succeeding deadline. Chancellor Willy Brandt got in touch with the Israeli government and was asked not to give in to the Arab blackmail. He also telephoned Prime Minister Sidki of Egypt and proposed that the terrorists should take their hostages to Cairo, from where the Israelis could be returned, but he was rebuffed, with Sidki arguing that this was not Egypt's affair and he could do nothing about it. The Egyptians were later to say that the West completely misunderstood Sidki's reply and that he was merely explaining that the Egyptian government was just as powerless as the Germans to obtain the release of the hostages before the Palestinians' demands had been met. To move them all to Cairo, they said, would simply have transferred the dilemma from Herr Brandt's lap to President Sadat's.

The Germans considered various ways of getting at the terrorists. Gas and chemical weapons were dismissed as unfeasible. There was a contingency plan to storm the Israeli quarters. But the Arabs seemed too well armed, too alert and too ruthless for that to succeed without the hostages being killed.

Finally it was decided to appear to give in. The Arabs and the hostages were flown in two helicopters to the military airfield at Furstenfeldbruck, where a Boeing 707 of Lufthansa was drawn up on the tarmac ostensibly to fly the whole bizarre party to Tunis. But the airfield was ringed with armored cars, machine guns and troops, and five police snipers were waiting for their targets.

The helicopters touched down on the brightly lit airfield at 10:35 P.M., each carrying a mixture of Arabs and Israelis—the Arabs armed with Kalashnikovs and grenades, the Israelis tied hand and foot. Before the rotor blades stopped one terrorist jumped from each helicopter and walked toward the Boeing. Immediately after the two men started to walk across the 165 yards between the airliner and the helicopters, two more terrorists jumped from the helicopters and ordered the pilot and copilot to get out. The first two men boarded the Boeing to make sure there were no ambushers inside—this plan had been considered by the police but had been discarded as being too dangerous. Having completed their inspection, they started to walk back to the helicopters. When they were halfway there the police snipers opened fire. Their first volley killed the two terrorists standing beside the helicopters and one of the men walking across the tarmac, but they missed the leader—presuambly the man named as Mohammed Masalhah—and he was able to dive for cover. The surviving terrorists immediately started to kill the hostages and to open fire on the control tower. One policeman was killed and the tower radio was put out of action. At 10:50 the police appealed to the terrorists over loudspeakers in German, English and Arabic to throw down their weapons and surrender. But the only answer was more shots.

At four minutes past midnight, after more armored cars had arrived from Munich, a terrorist jumped out of one of the helicopters, then turned and hurled a grenade into its cabin. At the same time another man, possibly the leader, emerged from the shadows where he had been concealed. Both men were shot by the snipers. But the grenade had set fire to the helicopter and it is probable that by this time the nine hostages were already dead. Firemen who arrived to try to put out the flames were shot at by the three surviving terrorists, but the armored cars now moved in and captured the three in and beside the undamaged helicopter. There was one other casualty, one of the volunteer helicopter pilots was shot in the lung and badly wounded.

There was a torrent of criticism of the way the Bavarian police had handled the affair. The Arabs accused them of duplicity and the rest of the world of inefficiency—a strange criticism to be leveled at Bavarians. Later, at a press conference, Herr Manfred Schreiber, Munich's Police Chief, defended his course of action, arguing that the hostages were practically doomed from the start. "They could have been saved only if their captors had made mistakes. Our chances of freeing them were virtually nil. . . . We had no influence on the Israeli government or on the terrorists."

Israel would not give in to Black September's demands and the terrorists would not free the hostages. "Some people say that it was police mistakes that caused the death of the hostages," Herr Schreiber said, "but it was the other way around. The hostages died because the terrorists made no mistakes." Dr. Bruno Merck, the Bavarian Interior Minister, supported the police chief when he was asked why the rescue attempt had failed. "Because," he said, "at the moment we fired there were not enough terrorists exposed. We had expected, nevertheless, that those who had not been shot would surrender in the shock of the gun battle. This didn't happen. . . . All we could do was to hope for a mistake. But these people are not amateurs."

Mrs. Golda Meir thanked the West German government for its efforts to free the Israelis. But there is no doubt that she was extremely displeased with the security arrangements at the Olympic Village. Three senior officials of Shin Bet—the Israeli Department of Internal Security—were fired. And, for their part, the Bavarian government absorbed the lessons and set up a special anti-terrorist force of marksmen, commandos, undercover men and technical experts. There were other consequences of the massacre. Germany clamped down on the Palestinian students and workers in her universities and factories. Relations between Germany and the Arab countries, particularly Egypt, became strained at a time when much effort had gone into restoring the relations which had been broken off when Nasser welcomed the East German Communist leader Walther Ulbricht to Egypt and the West Germans had retaliated by recognizing Israel. The Olympic Games were held up for one day and a service of remembrance held for the dead Israelis. Many people thought at the time the Games should have been canceled, but, in retrospect, it now seems that the decision to carry on was correct. Another, by now customary result was that seven weeks later two Black Septembrists hijacked a Boeing 727, Lufthansa Flight 615 from Damascus to Frankfurt, and held it for ransom until the three surviving terrorists from Munich were handed over to them at Zagreb airport, whereupon they all flew off to Libya, the terrorists' sanctuary.

But that was all in the future. On Furstenfeldbruck airfield in the early moments of September 6 the German authorities were faced with a scene of carnage as Israeli and Arab bodies lay together in death. It was at this moment that newspapermen covering the story were told by Herr Ahlers, the official government spokesman in Bonn, that all the hostages had been rescued unharmed. They filed their stories and there was universal jubilation. It was not until much later in the day that the Mayor of Munich, Herr Kronawitter, revealed that they had all been killed. This strange incident has never been explained properly, but it is thought that someone decided on the deception in order to gain time to think in a most desperate situation.

The next day an El Al flight carried ten of the dead sportsmen home to Israel along with the remaining fourteen members of the team, while the last of the dead, David Berger, was sent to Cleveland, Ohio, where his parents lived. Four days later the dead Black Septembrists were flown to Libya, where funeral prayers were said for them in Tripoli's main mosque. Libyan radio called them martyrs and heroes and the Voice of Palestine broadcast what it claimed to be the last will and testament of the terrorists, sent to the station a few hours before they burst into the Olympic Village. With it they sent five hundred dollars and thirty-seven marks, all they possessed, to be given to the Palestinian revolution. In their will, they said, "We are neither killers nor bandits. We are persecuted people who have no land and no homeland," and said that while they were skeptical of their chances of success they had been willing "to give up our lives from the very first moment. . . . This time we shall force them to know we are serious.

"We will the youth of the Arab nation to search for death so that life is given to them, their countries and their people. Each drop of blood spilled from you and from us will be oil to kindle this nation with flames of victory and liberation."

They apologized to world sports youth for interrupting the Games. "We are asking them to know that there is a people with a twenty-four-year-old case. . . . It would do no harm to the youth of the world to learn of our plight only in a few hours. We are not against any people, but why should our place here be taken by the flag of the occupiers . . . why should the whole world be having fun and entertainment while we suffer with all ears deaf to us?"

At Lod, where only three months before the Japanese terrorists had carried out their massacre, thousands of people stood in silence as the ten coffins were unloaded by soldiers and placed in military vehicles, each one with a guard of honor.

The dead sportsmen's families formed a square on the tarmac, standing with bowed heads as the army's Chief Chaplain recited their names and then started the prayer for the dead: "Hear, O Israel . . ."

It was at this moment that Israel declared war on the terrorists, universal and unconditional war to the death by all available means. Black September, by its very success at Munich, had insured that it would come under an attack so ferocious that its leaders would be shot down in their own homes and its agents harried to their deaths by bomb and pistol throughout Europe.

"The hands of Israel will know what to do," said Yosef Burg, the Minister of the Interior. "Israel's blood is not for the taking." And Mrs. Meir, speaking to the Knesset one week after Munich, gave a clear indication of what was going to happen. Israel would fight Arab terrorists wherever possible, she said. "We have no choice but to strike at them."

6 • The Wrath of God

I N FACT, Israel had already begun to strike back at the terrorists. After the PFLP had boasted of its responsibility for the Japanese massacre at Lod, attempts were made by the Israelis to assassinate the leadership of PFLP. But George Habash, sick with heart trouble, and Wadi Haddad, in the deepest hiding following the rocket attack on his apartment, could not be reached. The Israelis had to be content with Bassam Abu Sherif, whom they maimed with a letter bomb, and Ghassan Kanafani, PFLP's propagandist and number four in the party's hierarchy. He was blown to pieces by a bomb when he switched on the ignition of his car in Beirut on July 9, 1972. In one of the tragedies of this war, another innocent was killed, Kanafani's sixteen-year-old niece, who was walking toward the car when it exploded.

However, these attacks on PFLP leaders were not part of a

coordinated plan; they were acts of revenge for specific operations carried out by the terrorists—Kanafani signed his own
death warrant by announcing PFLP's responsibility for Lod—
and it was not until after Munich that the Israelis decided to
launch an anti-terrorist war designed to wipe out Black Sep-
tember/Fatah, PFLP and any other group that might act
against Israel. From the very start the Israelis made it clear
that they regarded Fatah and Black September one and the
same and that they would kill Fatah men as if they were Black
Septembrists.

Mrs. Meir called in Major General Aharon Yariv to run
the anti-terrorist campaign. Yariv had been a brilliant commander of military intelligence and now he became part of the
Prime Minister's office with sweeping powers, using both the
army and the secret service to hit at the terrorists. His organization came to be called "Mivtzan Elohim"—"The Wrath
of God." The Israelis have always believed in the policy of an
eye for an eye—and preferably two for one—and have officially
adopted the policy of massive retaliation. They are also experts
in terrorism. The Stern Gang and the Irgun Zvai Leumi, who
had fought the Arabs and the British under their badge of a
rifle gripped in a clenched fist with the motto "Only Thus,"
perpetrated some horrific acts of terrorism during the struggle
to establish the State of Israel: the assassination of Count Folke
Bernadotte, the blowing up of the King David Hotel, the hanging of two British sergeants in an orange grove and then booby-
trapping their bodies, and the massacre of Deir Yassin, in
which nearly two hundred innocent Arab villagers were slaughtered. Deir Yassin became the cry for revenge among the
Arabs and even today it is an emotive justification for Arab
terror. One may argue that the Arabs carried out equally appalling acts during that period, such as the ambushing of a medical
convoy on its way to the Hadassah Hospital on Mount Scopus,
in which some eighty doctors, nurses and professors were
killed, but that sort of argument carries no weight with the

Arabs. The circumstances of Deir Yassin were horrific enough
—without subsequent embroidering—to provide the Arabs with
a perpetual excuse for terror. The Israelis were also expert in
the construction of letter bombs. They sent one to a much
decorated British major in the Special Air Service, Roy Farran,
who had been acquitted by a court-martial of killing a young
member of the Stern Gang. The device was opened by Farran's
civilian bother, Rex, and he was killed. Other letter bombs were
sent to the German scientists who were working for Nasser,
developing jet aircraft, rockets and a rudimentary "dirty" atom
bomb made from radioactive waste. One of them blinded the
secretary of the German rocket expert Dr. Adolf Pilz. Another
killed an ex-SS man who was working in Cairo.

But the Arabs also had their letter-bomb experts, and it was
with dozens of these bombs posted from the most unlikely
places that the terrorists launched their next attack. On Tues-
day September 9, 1972, Dr. Ami Shachori, the forty-four-year-
old Agricultural Counselor at the Israeli Embassy in London,
returned to work after the long weekend of the Day of Atonement and found a pile of mail accumulated on his desk. He
had no fears of it. All parcels arriving at the embassy were
checked by the security guards and few people would want to
kill an agriculturalist who had devoted his life to improving
crops. He started to open his letters. He picked up one, a
thick, buff-colored envelope measuring six inches by three
which carried an Amsterdam postmark and had his name and
address written in ink. It exploded as he opened it. Most of the
blast funneled downward toward the desk and Dr. Shachori
escaped the worst effects of the initial explosion, but by the
worst possible piece of luck the blast shattered the desk and a
splinter drove into his heart and killed him.

The device works on the mousetrap principle. The spring of
a detonator is folded back and packed into the envelope with
a strip of plastic explosive weighing two or three ounces. When
the letter is opened, pressure on the spring is released and it

flies back to strike the detonator. This in turn sets off the explosive.

Dr. Shachori's death set off a search for similar bombs. Four more, made on the same principle with similar materials and the same postmark and same handwriting, were found addressed to individual members of the embassy. Another four were found addressed personally to the Ambassador, Mr. Michael Comay. But this was only the start of a flood of letter bombs, all the same, all posted from Holland, addressed to Israeli embassies all over the world. Thirty-one were intercepted during the next two weeks in eight different countries—eight in London, six in Ottawa, five in Vienna, three in New York, three in Geneva, two in Paris, one in Montreal, one in Brussels and two in Israel. One of those posted to New York was intended for Mr. Josef Tekoah, Israel's Ambassador to the United Nations, and one of those that arrived in Israel was addressed to Mr. Shimon Peres, Israel's Minister of Transport. A few days later five more letter bombs arrived in Australia destined for Israeli diplomats. Others were sent to Israeli embassies at Kinshasa, Buenos Aires and Phnom Penh. Alerted by the death of Dr. Shachori, the Israeli security guards and postal authorities around the world were able to pick out the bombs before they could do any more damage. But this was not the end of it. There was another wave of letter bombs, posted this time from India and addressed to individual Jews. They were in colored envelopes, mostly pink, and carried stamps far in excess of the value required. One was sent to the woman heading the Hadassah organization in New York, and in the first eleven days of November fourteen were sent to individual Jews and Jewish organizations in Britain. One of them severely wounded Mr. Vivian Prins, a London diamond merchant, and another casualty was caused when a bomb blew up in New York and wounded a local post office worker. One macabre letter bomb was sent to a Dutch Jew. It was a poison-gas letter containing forty grams of cyanide in powder form, like fine grains of salt. In chemical composition with oxygen it would have produced poison gas, but it was detected in time. One of the problems with letter bombs is that some postal services are not all that fast and bombs posted in India destined for South America sometimes took weeks to arrive, so that they were turning up long after it was thought they had all been accounted for—forty-two were intercepted in Bombay. One of the late arrivals blew up, wounding the police technician who was handling it in Santiago, Chile, on January 24, 1973, and another one arrived at the Israeli Embassy in Guatemala long after the others in its batch had been delivered.

Three other letter bombs were posted from the Israeli town of Kiryat Shemona addressed to President Nixon, Secretary of State Rogers and Defense Secretary Laird. These were intercepted by suspicious Israeli postal workers and it is thought that they were either smuggled across the nearby Lebanese border or posted by a local Arab. The letter bombs were all attributed to Black September.

The Israelis could not be expected to remain passive under this onslaught and they soon returned it in kind. On October 24 a series of letter bombs posted in Belgrade began to land on the desks of Palestinian resistance leaders in Lebanon, Egypt, Libya and Algeria. The Fatah representative in Algiers, Abu Khalil, was injured when one blew up in his face. In Libya, Mustafa Awadh Abu Zeid was blinded by a parcel bomb. He was later flown to London for treatment.

Two bombs addressed to Palestinian businessmen in Beirut blew up, blinding a postman and injuring the secretary of one of the Palestinians. In Cairo one of three letter bombs addressed to the Palestine Liberation Organization exploded as it was being examined at Cairo airport, seriously injuring a security officer.

It was at this time that Mrs. Golda Meir, asked at a lunch given by Israeli journalists why Israel had taken no action against the Munich terrorists, replied: "Suppose some acts have been done, only you, the press, don't know about it. Would you expect me to tell this intimate forum what, if anything, has been done against terrorism?"

In fact, one of the first measures to be taken against the terrorists was preventative. Israeli embassies all around the world were turned into miniature fortresses capable of withstanding full-scale assaults from Black September commandos. Orders were issued from Tel Aviv that Israeli diplomats must not rely on local police forces for their protection but had to take measures of self-protection unparalleled in the history of diplomacy.

Every British embassy has a few small arms in the care of the military attaché, who, among his other duties, is in charge of the protection of the building. He usually has a few retired noncommissioned officers who have joined the Foreign Service to act as guards, but apart from them and any sporting diplomat's shotguns British embassies look to local governments for protection. United States embassies have their traditional Marine guards, who are armed and tough, but even the American precautions cannot be compared with those now being taken by the Israelis. Their embassy in London is in Kensington Palace Green, in that distinguished avenue of embassies alongside Kensington Palace, where starched nannies wheel their pampered charges and a top-hatted custodian politely inquires a visitor's business before swinging up the barrier that blocks the avenue to vulgar traffic. But the Israeli Embassy, just a hundred yards along the avenue from the Egyptian Consulate, is a different proposition. It is shut in by a steel fence and the only way in is through a remote-controlled gate. There is usually a car outside with a couple of hard-looking young men tinkering with its engine. It must be the best-maintained car in London. The visitor walks past their scrutiny and presses a buzzer on the gate. A voice then issues from a microphone on the gate demanding to know the visitor's name, business and the name of the diplomat he wishes to see. If the answer is satisfactory a buzzer sounds and the door swings open, allowing the visitor to walk up the garden path while the gate swings shut behind him.

There is a further scrutiny by voice and through a peephole at the front door, which is also electrically controlled. Then, having got past that barrier, the visitor enters the front hall and is immediately conscious of the number of watchful young men who seem to be just sitting around, doing nothing. One's movements become deliberate and slow. It would be unwise to excite suspicion. After further interrogation by the receptionist comes the search, first of one's briefcase and then of one's person. Even ballpoint pens are examined to make sure that they really are pens and not killing mechanisms. Only then is the visitor allowed to enter the anteroom to wait for the diplomat he has arranged to see and all the time he is under surveillance by closed-circuit television. It is no wonder that most people choose to meet their Israeli friends outside the embassy. As one Israeli diplomat put it: "Our embassies are no longer pleasant places to visit—even for our friends. But they are the new front line."

In Paris, the Israeli Embassy is in the Rue Rabelais, just two blocks from the Elysée Palace, and there stocks of Uzzi submachine guns have been built up for the squad of guards to use if the Arabs launch an attack. Thick steel doors have been installed and an armor-plated barrier has divided the small reception hall, with the outer portion forming a box in which a visitor can be electronically, verbally and visually scanned before being accepted or rejected or, if he proves to be a terrorist, killed.

In Cyprus, where the Israeli Ambassador, Rahamin Timor, missed death by seconds when Black September terrorists planted a bomb outside his home on April 9, 1973, the embassy is in a block of offices in the center of Nicosia. There is only one way up, a small elevator which opens onto a landing scanned by closed-circuit television. The front door leads into a boxlike inspection room which could very easily become a

95

killing room, and visitors are questioned from behind a close-meshed steel grill. If the visitor answers the questions satisfactorily, a buzzer sounds and an armored door opens into a reception area containing half a dozen hefty young men and several of those spectacular bronzed girls that Israel breeds. From there, padlocked gates lead off to the Ambassador's office. They are locked each time someone passes through. These are only the outward precautions, visible to anyone who visits an Israeli embassy anywhere in the world. There are other, hidden precautions. Every embassy contains enough pistols, submachine guns and grenades to equip a platoon of infantry. They have also had steel and concrete poured into them, so that they are now able to withstand a form of attack perfected by the IRA—the car bomb.

At the same time as they began to build their embassy fortresses the Israelis instituted the most stringent checks on travelers flying to Tel Aviv. Squads of searchers go through the baggage of every passenger flying by El Al. Aerosol cans are given trial squirts to see if they really do contain what it says on their labels. Tape recorders are played and then returned with the batteries removed. And at Lod airport passengers leaving Israel are faced by a long line of tables manned by men armed with screwdrivers who take apart any electrical or mechanical equipment being carried on board. The last time I went through, my typewriter was stripped down. It is possible to carry parts of a pistol in a portable typewriter, with the roller concealing the pistol's barrel. I must admit that the typewriter worked better than before, once it had been reassembled, but I had a few nasty moments when my searcher discovered some Fatah posters and Lebanese banknotes in my briefcase. It took a lot of talking to explain that I really was a writer engaged on research and not a Fatah supporter.

The necessity for the precautions in the air is self-evident—even if they were not to the American woman who had a large ornamental candle confiscated by the authorities when she told them it had been given to her by a "very nice Arab in the Old City of Jerusalem." And if you ask an Israeli if the massive precautions at his embassies are necessary, he will refer you to Black September's statement after one of their operational groups occupied the Israeli Embassy in Bangkok in December 1972 and held six Israeli diplomats hostage: "Israeli embassies anywhere in the world," said Black September, "are to be regarded as Palestinian territory."

The precautions against car bombs are certainly justified. At least two attempts have been made. One started in the Lebanese Fatah base at Nahar al Bared when Mohammed Tabab, a Jordanian, and Sakar Mahmoud al Khalil, a Palestinian, set out for Europe in a Mercedes into which thirty-five pounds of plastic explosives had been packed and wired for detonation. Their destination: the Israeli Embassy in Paris. The Israelis knew all about this car and had it tracked all the way to La Grave in the French Hautes-Alpes. The Israelis could have acted earlier, but they decided to make the French police act on this one because they had not previously been overly zealous on cracking down in Paris. When the French did pick up the car they found not only the explosives but a spare license plate—CDK 59, a diplomatic number allocated to the Israeli Embassy in Paris. Following the arrest of these two terrorists, the French police picked up a Palestinian, Jamil Abdel Hakim, and a British woman doctor, Diane Campbell-Lefevre, aged thirty-one, who had worked in Palestinian refugee camps. The French police held her for five days and then put her on a plane for London. On the plane she was interviewed by a British correspondent who quoted her as saying: "If you had seen these poor people as I have, you could not fail to sympathize with the cause.

"I worked and lived among the Palestinians and grew to love them. When you know the shocking killings done by the Israelis since 1948, you don't doubt the wisdom of my movement's policies." What work had she been engaged in? "I can't say

97

too much, my movement does not like press coverage; they don't understand concepts like freedom of the press in the West. I'm not really free to say anything." She did however agree, "I handled explosives." A few days later she denied everything.

These preventative measures of safeguarding the embassies and airliners and of tipping off European governments about operations planned by the Arabs were one aspect of the measures that Golda Meir had spoken about. Another aspect, more direct and more deadly, is the war of assassination which General Yariv's men launched throughout Europe. Until the killings at Lod and Munich there had been an unwritten agreement between the Israelis and the Arabs that they would not indulge in wiping out each other's agents abroad. But, as we have seen, after Lod the Israelis did their best to wipe out the leadership of the PFLP. After Munich, Fatah too became fair game.

The first man to die was Wael Zwaiter, officially a clerk at Libya's embassy in Rome, but actually Fatah's representative in the city. He was shot twelve times by two men armed with .22 pistols—the Wrath of God's favorite weapon—as he entered the elevator leading to his apartment. The Israelis say that he was Black September's man in Rome and was therefore one of the men responsible for the Lod massacre, the booby-trapped tape recorder and a number of other terrorist operations originating in Rome. At this time Black September, basing itself on the original Razd setup, had made Rome its headquarters. There was no doubt in the Israelis' minds that the Fatah representative had to be deeply involved in all the terrorist activity emanating from Rome. Zwaiter's friends, however, maintain that he was a peaceful intellectual whose "main dream was the revival of Arab culture which had once flourished from Alexandria to Baghdad and from Spain to Sicily and which had enriched the entire civilized world." But Zwaiter was an apologist for the Munich affair and even suggested that the Israelis had plotted to have the hostages killed so that they could gain political advantage from it. That alone was enough to condemn him to death. The next man to die was Mahmoud Hamshari, the PLO representative in Paris. The Israelis staked out his apartment in Paris, noting the time each morning when his French wife, Marie-Claude, took their daughter, Amina, to nursery school. One Israeli, posing as an Italian journalist, made contact with Hamshari on the pretext of interviewing him. While they were meeting at a café another member of the execution squad took an impression of the lock on the door of Hamshari's apartment. The "Italian" arranged a further meeting with Hamshari and this time, using a key made from the impression, the second Israeli walked into the apartment and fitted an electronically controlled bomb into the base of Hamshari's telephone. The next day the phone rang just after Mrs. Hamshari and Amina had left. Hamshari answered it. A voice at the other end said: "This is the Italian journalist who has a rendezvous with you today. That's really you, Monsieur Hamshari?" The Palestinian replied, "Yes, this is Mahmoud Hamshari." And as soon as he said that the telephone exploded. He lived long enough to tell the police what had happened and they were able to piece together the electronic device which had killed him. The trigger mechanism was based on the same sort of mechanism as that fitted to scrambler telephones.

A similar device, this time activated by a radio signal, accounted for Hussein Bashir in his room at the Olympic Hotel in Nicosia the following month. Bashir, a thirty-six-year-old Palestinian, had arrived on the island equipped with a Syrian passport, a Lebanese *laissez passer* and an identity card giving his position as leader of the forty-strong Fatah contingent on the island. He made regular visits to the island and, as usual, he booked into the Olympic Hotel, a small establishment on President Makarios Avenue much favored by Arabs. Two days after his arrival an explosion in the early hours of the morning rocked the hotel. Policemen in the nearby station house—no strangers to explosions in the night—ran to the hotel and kicked down the jammed door of Bashir's room. A bomb had been put under his mattress and detonated by a short-range radio transmission. Bashir had been blown to pieces. Cyprus had been a neutral ground for both Arabs and Israelis. It had the same sort of status as Lisbon had during World War II when Allied and Axis intelligence agents ate in the same restaurants, drank in the same bars and slept with the same girls. Cyprus had achieved this position because of its geographic location, only thirty minutes by air from Beirut and only forty-five minutes from Tel Aviv. It was the place where the Arab and Israeli world met and people could change sides by changing planes at the airport. But with Bashir's death it was no longer a question of live and let live but of kill and be killed. In March, two months after Bashir's death, Simha Gilzer, a veteran of Irgun Zvai Leumi who the Israelis claimed was an innocent businessman but was in fact a senior security officer, was shot down on the steps of the Nicosia Palace Hotel just a stone's throw from where Bashir had been killed. This was followed by the simultaneous attempt to blow up the Israeli Ambassador and an attack on an El Al jet at Nicosia airport. The attackers, members of PFLP working under the name of the Arab Nationalist Youth Organization for the Liberation of Palestine, almost got the Ambassador but made a mess of their getaway and of the attack at the airport. An Israeli security guard shot two of them dead and seven others were arrested after a wild car chase and gun fight. It was a very confused affair, but what seems to have happened is that the terrorists split into two groups. One, three strong, drove to Ambassador Timor's home, an apartment in a three-story building in a pleasant residential area in Nicosia. They timed their arrival to coincide with Mr. Timor's normal after-lunch walk. But he had set out a few minutes early. A small, neat man who had previously been in charge of aid programs to African countries, he later told me: "I escaped by the skin of my teeth."

The attackers drove up, shot the Cypriot policeman guarding the house in the back, severely wounding him, and then dumped forty pounds of dynamite by the front door. However, they did not put the bomb close enough to the house and, according to a Cypriot explosives expert, it was made by someone "who had absolutely no idea about explosives," so, although it knocked a hole in the structure, it did more damage to the terrorists' car than to the house. They had to abandon their car and seize another at gunpoint from a passing motorist, but by this time the police were on the scene. They chased the car, shot it up, wounded one of the terrorists and arrested the other two, forcing them to lie on their backs in the middle of the road with their hands behind their heads. Meanwhile, another group, using a car and a Land-Rover, crashed through the barriers at the airport and drove toward an El Al Viscount which had just disembarked its passengers from Tel Aviv. As they careered toward the plane stitching it with machine-gun bullets, an Israeli guard and police opened fire on them. It was the security guard who foiled the attack. He killed one of the terrorists with his pistol and then fell on the floor of the plane as if shot. But he was merely luring the attackers closer. They fell for the bait, moved in, and he jumped up with an Uzzi machine pistol blazing. He killed another one and sent the Land-Rover crashing into a mobile generator. The survivors were arrested. Later an Israeli security official said: "Let's say we knew the Arabs would strike, so we brought in help from Israel and warned the Cypriots. We were at the airport early this morning waiting for something to happen."

When the Cypriot police searched the Land-Rover they found the now customary declaration of apology and intent from the terrorists, who had obviously set out to try a hijack. It read: "We are the new pilots and commanders of this plane. Please don't force us to use violence. Remain in your seats. We are representatives of the Arab Nationalist Youth Organization for the Liberation of Palestine. To the friendly people of Cyprus:

We are very sorry for the fight on your beautiful island. We did not start this fight. We are only struggling to regain our land and our homes."

When they appeared before a magistrate's court two months later, the seven survivors caused an uproar, shouting at the prosecutor and threatening a police witness. One of them yelled at the prosecutor: "We did what we did for the ideal of the Palestine Revolution. By detaining us you are preventing us from fighting against Israel. How can Cyprus say that it was a friend of the Arabs?" This is the sort of blindly illogical logic that is always used by the terrorists and their supporters, not only in justifying their actions but in glorifying them. The fact that they had cold-bloodedly shot a Cypriot policeman and endangered the lives of many innocent people counted for nothing. All that mattered to them was to strike at the Israelis as often and as hard as they could. If innocents suffered, then it was a misfortune of war.

Four months later a KLM Jumbo jet carrying 287 people was crossing Iraq after taking off from Beirut for New Delhi and Tokyo when the captain reported by radio: "Two sky-jackers are standing with pistols in my back." The terrorists, who identified themselves as members of the Arab Nationalist Youth Organization for the Liberation of Palestine, ordered the pilot to fly to Nicosia and when it landed they demanded the release of their seven colleagues. This was refused at the time and the Jumbo took off again, touching down in Libya—where the hijackers were rebuffed—before flying on to Malta, where they released their hostages before flying south again to surrender in Dubai. President Makarios of Cyprus ordered the release of the seven terrorists, and they left the island as free men, wearing smart Beirut-style suits, smiling handsomely and giving the victory sign.

The war of assassination had also spread throughout Europe. In September 1972, Mr. Ophir Zadok, an Israeli security official at the embassy in Brussels, received a telephone call from a man who said he had information about a terrorist plot against the embassy. The caller, who gave his name as Mohammed Ahmed Rabbah, refused to go to the embassy but proposed a meeting at Prince's Café in De Brouckere Square in the center of Brussels. Zadok agreed and went to the café, whose owner, Jean Redding, later described what happened: "I noticed a man looking like an Arab pacing the pavement as if waiting for someone. He was soon joined by another man of the same type and they both came into the café. Another man had come in and was sitting in a dark corner without ordering. The two Arab-looking men stood there for a moment, one of them nodding toward the seated man as if pointing him out. Then he walked out in a hurry. I then heard five shots and saw the man sitting alone stand up, covered in blood. He staggered toward the front door and collapsed on a seat. The gunman, holding a light machine gun, rushed past him into the street and disappeared." Zadok had been seriously wounded by two bullets, but he recovered.

In November a Syrian journalist, Khodr Kannou, was shot dead in Paris by Black September. It seems that he was a double agent and as a result of information he had passed to the Israelis several Black Septembrists had been eliminated. Now it was his turn. In January 1973, Baruch Cohen, the chief Israeli intelligence agent in Madrid, went to a café on the Grand Via in Madrid to meet an Arab contact who had promised to give Cohen the names of the most politically active Arab students at the university. The contact put his hand in his pocket ostensibly to bring out the list of names, but he brought out a pistol instead. Cohen dived for cover but he was hit four times and died. In April, Dr. Bassel Rauf Kubeisy, an Iraqi professor of law at the American University in Beirut who was also a leading member of PFLP, was returning to his hotel in the shadow of the Madeleine Church in Paris soon after midnight. An eyewitness said he was walking fast, apparently trying to get away from two young men following him. The two men caught up with him. He looked around, terrified, and tried to run, crying out: *"Non! Non! Ne faites pas cela."* But the two men produced .22 pistols and shot him ten times. The following day PFLP issued a statement announcing that Kubeisy had been one of its leaders and was on a mission for the organization when he was killed.

Later the same month, Ahmed Aboussan, an agent of Razd, was fast asleep in his hotel bedroom when the door opened and a bomb was tossed in. Aboussan died instantly. At the end of the same month Vittorio Olivares, an Italian working for El Al in Rome, was shot twice in the stomach and killed by an Arab armed with a long-barreled pistol fitted with a silencer. The shooting took place outside a department store in the busy city center, and as the gunman ran away he fired several shots in the air to keep the crowd away, but he was eventually stopped and disarmed by two policemen. He gave his name as Zaharia Abu Saleh and said he had been sent to Rome by Black September with orders to shoot Olivares.

Then, on June 29, the Israelis carried out a real coup. They blew Mohammed Boudia to pieces. Boudia, according to *L'Aurore* (a well-informed Paris daily), was the boss of the Black September network in France. He was wanted by the Italian police for the blowing up of the oil terminal at Trieste and had been named by Evelyne Barges, a Frenchwoman picked up by the Israelis on a sabotage mission in Tel Aviv, as the mastermind of her group. Boudia had a complicated background. He was an Algerian who belonged to a clandestine Marxist group opposed to the regime of Colonel Houari Boumedienne. He was manager of the Théâtre de l'Ouest and with Mahmoud Hamshari had wide contacts among the Left Bank intelligentsia in Paris, where they recruited French militants for Black September operations. Boudia's specialty was seducing French girls and then getting them to carry out terrorist missions. It was his sexual activities that got him killed. When the French police pulled him out of the wreckage of his Renault

16, which had exploded when he switched on the ignition, they thought at first he had been killed by a bomb he had been carrying into his car, for, according to the testimony of one of his girl friends, he had spent the night with her some distance away and if he had driven from her apartment to the scene of the explosion it would have been impossible for an ignition bomb to have been planted—it would have exploded as soon as he switched it on outside her house. But they later learned that Boudia had in fact spent the night with another woman, who lived in the street where the car exploded, the Rue des Fosses-St.-Bernard. His car had been parked there all night and it had been easy for his killers to wire up the bomb. He had been, said *L'Aurore,* near the top of the Israeli list of *"les hommes à abattre."* Certainly the Israelis, without admitting the killing, took care that it was thought to be justified. They circulated photostatic copies of handwritten confessions by some of his girl saboteurs naming him as their terrorist boss.

It could not be expected that Boudia's grisly death would go unavenged. Three days later Colonel Yosef Alon, the deputy military attaché at the Israeli Embassy in Washington, was shot five times in his front garden as he and his wife, Deborah, returned from a party. Mrs. Alon was standing inside the porch waiting for him as he put their car away. When she heard the shots she ran inside to telephone the police and then she went outside to find her husband dying on his carefully tended lawn. Both his parents had died in a Nazi concentration camp but he survived to become one of Israel's best pilots. His job in Washington was to supervise the supply of Phantoms and Skyhawks to the Israeli air force. The Washington police, unwilling to admit that the war of assassination had arrived in its bailiwick, suggested that he might have been shot by one of the capital's ordinary thugs. But the Arabs were in no doubt about who was responsible. In Cairo the Voice of Palestine proudly proclaimed that Alon had been "executed" in retaliation for the killing of Boudia, and in Beirut the terrorists' mouthpiece, *Al Moharrer,* announced: "The fact that the arm of the Palestinians has reached the American stronghold in Washington is another piece of evidence that there is nothing—absolutely nothing—which will stop the Palestinian people from expanding the scope of the war against its enemies." The Israelis had no doubts either. At Alon's funeral, General Dayan vowed: "We shall continue to hit the terrorists wherever they can be reached."

That vow was acted on three weeks later at Lillehammer, Norway, when a thirty-year-old Moroccan waiter named Ahmed Bouchki was shot dead by thirteen bullets from a .22 pistol as he was walking home from the cinema with his pregnant Norwegian wife. But this is an operation that went wrong. It was claimed that Bouchki was a Black Septembrist, but it seems likely that his killers got the wrong man and that he was innocent of terrorism. Then the Norwegian police traced the killers to the home of Yigal Eyal, security chief of the Israeli Embassy. The police broke in, technically a breach of diplomatic immunity, and arrested two Israelis they found hiding in the house. Four more Israelis were arrested at Oslo airport as they were attempting to leave the country. Norwegian officials said that they were carrying forged passports.

There was a great diplomatic furor over this incident. The Israelis protested about the breach of diplomatic immunity, while the Norwegians, enraged by the Israelis' arrogance in using their country for killing and frightened that it might become an Arab-Israeli battleground, expelled Yigal Eyal. Mrs. Meir told her cabinet that she had demanded a full report on the affair and later spoke of Israel's worldwide battle against terrorism. She told a convention of religious Zionists from America: "You cannot know and the people of Israel cannot know the details of how many Jews or Israelis are alive today because of our ability to prevent tragedies and horrors planned by terrorist gangs all over the world."

But Mrs. Meir's impassioned words did not stop the Norwegians from putting the Israeli execution team on trial. One of them, the Swedish-born Mrs. Marianne Gladnikoff, spilled the beans. She told the court that she had unwittingly joined a group of about fifteen people in Tel Aviv whose mission was to find and kill a member of the Black September organization in Norway. The man they were after was Ali Hassan Salameh. Five of the group were given prison sentences ranging from one to five and a half years. One thing is certain: there will be no hijackings by the Israelis to secure their release, for the Israelis play this game by the old-fashioned rules of espionage. Curiously enough, they may not have been as far out in their selection of target as the Norwegians at first thought, for during the trial an obituary notice appeared in a Moroccan newspaper which described Bouchki as a "fervent fighter for the Arab cause."

The "tragedies and horrors" involving innocent people of which Mrs. Meir spoke continued in a sort of macabre counterpoint to the war between the professional killers. On December 28, 1972, Mr. Rehavam Amir, the Israeli Ambassador in Bangkok, and his wife put on their evening dress and drove through a city festooned with lanterns and flags and ringing with the sound of temple bells to attend the investiture of Crown Prince Vijiralongkorn, the heir to the throne. Sometime later, Private Sunchai Pienkana of the Thai police, who was on guard at the embassy, saw two men in white tie and tails open the gate and walk into the embassy compound. "They bowed and smiled to me." He thought they were diplomats returning from the investiture until he noticed two other men carrying submachine guns climb over the wall. They were members of Black September. The four men rounded up all the Thais and told them to "Go! Go!" Sunchai ran to a telephone to give the alarm, and the four terrorists took over the embassy, bolting the front door, shutting the windows and taking six Israeli diplomats hostage, including Mr. Simon Avimor, the Israeli Ambassador to Cambodia, who was visiting Thailand. The hostages were forced at gunpoint up to the second floor of the three-story white brick embassy and their captors threw out a note in which they said: "The Zionist occupation of Palestine is criminal and inhuman." The note went on to say that any violence or treachery would cause the death of the hostages, "a disaster for which the local government would shoulder the responsibility." Ambassador Amir, the Thai Prime Minister, Marshal Thanom Kittikachorn, and the Interior Minister, General Praphas Charasathien, hurried to the embassy from the investiture and there they learned the terrorists' demands: Thirty-six leading terrorists held in Israeli prisons, including Kozo Okamoto, Rima Tannous and Therese Halsa, must be set free or else the hostages would be killed and the embassy blown up. There was no chance that the Israeli government would agree to these demands. Its policy has always been that no matter what happened, no matter who was killed, it would never give in to blackmail. This policy stems from the Nazi slaughter of six million Jews; most of them walked to the gas chambers without a struggle. After that holocaust the Jews said never again, never again will we give in without fighting; never again will we give in to blackmail. This was their policy at Munich. It was also to be their policy at Bangkok. After it was all over, Mr. Abba Eban, Israel's Foreign Secretary, said giving in to the terrorists' demands was "at no time even considered."

It seemed certain that the hostages were doomed, but the Thai authorities began a beautifully Oriental series of negotiations with the Black Septembrists and they were supported by the Egyptian Ambassador, Mustapha el Essawy, acting on the direct instructions of President Sadat. Between them they wore down the terrorists, and when the Thais offered them safe conduct to the airport and a special aircraft to any destination they chose, on condition that they released the hostages, they agreed.

They left for the airport in a shabby blue-and-white bus, taking their six prisoners with them. All the hostages, two of whom were women, were bound with rope and they were not untied until the terrorists handed them over and boarded a DC-8 of Thai Airways to fly to Cairo. Ambassador el Essawy, who had done so much to save the situation, flew with the Black Septembrists as guarantee for their safe conduct.

When she was released, Mrs. Ruth Hadas, who had been held hostage along with her husband, Nitzan, First Secretary at the embassy, did a little jig, a cigarette in one hand, a drink in he other, and said: "I didn't know it was so good to be alive."

It was a triumph of sanity and humanity. But in the eyes of Black September's militants it was an appalling failure. The Bangkok terrorists had shown weakness, they had not carried out their threats, they had not killed. Therefore, the militants argued, Black September had lost face, had lost credence. Nobody would take any notice of them if this failure was not redeemed either by making the enemy lose an equal amount of face or by blood. And so an operation was mounted which would once again change the rules of the game. It was to end in the Khartoum massacre.

7 • Kill and Counterkill

A BLINDING SANDSTORM sprang up over the Egyptian desert on February 21, 1973, and so confused the air traffic control system in Cairo—which must be one of the most inefficient in the world—that it sent a Libyan Boeing 727 on the regular short-haul run from Benghazi to Cairo right past the airport, out over the Pyramids, then through the Egyptian army's radar screen defending the Suez Canal and on to the Israeli-occupied Sinai, where, a few minutes later, Israeli Phantoms shot it down into the desert, where it crashed and burned and 106 people were killed.

The Israelis pleaded that they had tried to make contact with the airliner and force it to land but that its French pilot had refused their demand and that they therefore had no option but to shoot it down because Black September had threatened on a number of occasions to hijack a plane and turn it into a kamikaze bomb, diving it into the heart of Tel Aviv. But they were less than honest in their explanations of what had happened. It was proved, for instance, from the tape of the pilot's anguished appeals to the Cairo radio tower that the Israeli pilots had not made contact with him before shooting him down and one of the fighter pilots later admitted that the Boeing was turning, heading back to Egypt, when it was attacked, about ten miles inside Israeli-held territory.

The world was horrified. No Israeli reasoning could wipe out the effect of the pictures of broken bodies smoking in the wreckage of the airliner. It seemed that the Israelis were themselves adopting Black September tactics and that their policy of "Never Again" had spilled over into naked aggression against innocent people. In Cairo there were horrific scenes at the morgue when the bodies were returned in rough wooden boxes and the families of the dead, grieving as only Arabs can grieve, scrabbled for bits of flesh to bury. In Libya the crowds at the mass funeral of fifty-five of the victims called on Qaddafi to give them revenge and the Libyan government issued a statement which said that "by all objective standards the deliberate shooting down of a civilian airliner cannot be allowed to pass unpunished."

All this was given great display in the Arab newspapers. What was not reported was that the Libyan mob attacked Egyptian offices because, while they reserved most of their fury for the Israelis, they also blamed the Egyptians for their inefficiency in sending the airliner the wrong way. But this did not help the Israelis. Although their fear of Black September fanaticism was appreciated, the world could not excuse an act which, outside the beleaguered mentality of the Israelis, seemed at best hasty and unnecessary, and at worst a murder of innocents on a par with the massacre at Lod. The fact that it was carried out officially, by the government and not by a fanatic dedicated to terrorism, made it worse. The Arabs were not slow in gathering in this propaganda windfall. I was in Cairo at the time and, apart from the whipped-emotion of the masses, senior officials were gleeful about the effect the tragedy was having on Israel's position in the world. Realization of the great damage done to their nation's reputation overseas spread slowly among the Israelis and in the Knesset a resolution was passed which, while it expressed profound sorrow at the loss of life, nevertheless asserted that the Israeli armed forces had acted with concern for the security of the state. The resolution "vigorously rejected attempts to impute to Israel or its army any spurious blame for the catastrophe." Spurious or not, the world in general did blame Israel for the catastrophe and the Arabs began to feel that for the the first time they had redressed the balance of world opinion which had been so weighted against them by Lod and Munich.

But then, a week later, came Khartoum and, at a stroke, all the advantage accruing to the Arabs from the shooting down of the Libyan airliner was wiped out by an atrocity which was largely organized by the Libyans themselves.

I was talking with an Egyptian who was very close to President Sadat when the news of Khartoum came through. He shook his head in disbelief and said in anguish: "We always do it. No sooner do we gain an advantage than we destroy it ourselves. No sooner do we take a step forward than we hurl ourselves backward. I often think that there has to be an Israeli directing these operations. Only that would explain how we can be so self-destructive." This was an opinion which I heard expressed many times by responsible Egyptians. "The Israelis are behind it," they said. "They are organizing these atrocities to make us look like savages to the rest of the world."

But it was not like that. The Khartoum affair had nothing to do with the Libyan airliner and it was certainly not planned by the Israelis. It was a Black September operation run from the joint Fatah-PLO office in Khartoum with the backing of President Qaddafi of Libya. It had a number of origins. There was the failure at Bangkok which had to be wiped off the slate.

There was the realization that the Israelis would never give in to blackmail if their own people were held as hostages and therefore the next batch of hostages would have to be foreigners, and preferably important foreigners. There was the threat which had been made by King Faisal of Saudi Arabia to stop collecting taxes for the PLO—and consequently for Black September—from the Palestinians working in his country, so therefore he would have to be shown the power of Black September. There was the growing anger among the Arabs because of American support of the Israelis. And there was Colonel Qaddafi's fury toward President Nimeiry of the Sudan for refusing to allow a Libyan airborne force to pass through his country to help President Amin of Uganda in his mini-war against the supporters of the deposed Milton Obote.

All these factors came together in a simple, bloody equation on the night of March 1, 1973. The sandstorm in which the Libyan Boeing had wandered over the Suez was still blowing, and in Khartoum, dusty at the best of times, the air was full of gritty sand that made life uncomfortable and tempers short.

But at the Saudi Arabian Embassy nobody worried too much about the sand. There was a splendid party going, a farewell party given by the Saudi Ambassador for America's Deputy Chief of Mission, Mr. George Curtis Moore, a popular figure in the diplomatic community. The American Ambassador, Mr. Cleo Noel was there and so was Mr. Raymond Etherington-Smith, the British Ambassador. It was thought that Emperor Haile Selassie of neighboring Ethiopia might also put in an appearance. It was, for those people who believe a diplomat's life is one of easy parasitism, a typical high-level "cookie-pusher" affair—bright chatter, diplomats' wives eying their rivals' dresses, several people with serious business to do talking quietly in a corner, the host receiving his guests in a hand-shaking line. It was all very normal, quite pleasant, a little boring for those on the duty list who would rather have been elsewhere. Etherington-Smith made his excuses to his host and left early; he had to meet Mr. Anthony Kershaw, Britain's Under Secretary of State, who was arriving at the airport for an official visit to the Sudan.

It was a meeting which saved Etherington-Smith's life, for he was on the list of those to be taken hostage and killed by the Black September group which stormed into the embassy while the party was in full swing.

Some of the people at the party escaped over the garden wall as the Black Septembrists rushed in, brandishing their Kalashnikovs; others were told to leave by the terrorists. When the panic died down, the embassy grew quiet, with five men remaining in the terrorists hands: the Saudi Ambassador and the Jordanian chargé d'affaires, and Mr. Cleo Noel, the American Ambassador to the Sudan, Mr. George Curtis Moore, his chargé d'affaires, for whom the party had been given, and M. Guy Eid, the Belgian chargé d'affaires. The terrorists then made their demands. They wanted the Jordanians to release Abu Daoud and the sixteen Black Septembrists captured with him, they wanted the United States to release Sirhan Sirhan, the killer of Senator Robert Kennedy, they wanted Israel to release the Arab women terrorists held in Israeli jails and they wanted Germany to release its Baader-Meinhof prisoners. Otherwise, they said, the hostages would be killed. Negotiations went on throughout the night and the next day. The Sudanese authorities played the situation coolly. The army was kept out of sight and there was only a screen of policemen around the embassy. At one point one of the gang showed himself on a balcony casually tossing a grenade from one hand to another. The terrorists' leader allowed a doctor into the embassy to treat one of the Americans who had been hurt in the initial attack, and he asked the doctor to telephone Mrs. Moore to assure her that no harm would befall her husband if their demands were met. As the day wore on they whittled down those demands, asking only for the release of Abu Daoud and Sirhan Sirhan. But neither the Jordanians nor the Americans would give in to them. At a press conference in Washington, President Nixon said that America "cannot and will not pay blackmail."

By now the Sudanese authorities were taking a tougher line. An antitank gun was lined up against the main entrance of the embassy. It had reached the stage where the terrorists had to give up or kill their hostages. They killed. A burst of shots was heard just after nine in the evening and then the telephone rang in the American embassy and the Black September leader announced: "We have executed the two Americans and the Belgian." The Saudi Ambassador, who was later to be released with the Jordanian chargé, said that when Mr. Noel was told he was going to be shot, the American turned to him and said: "I'm very sorry it has turned out this way, but I want you to know it is not your fault." He was very composed, very brave, and even at that stage had the courtesy to thank the Saudi Ambassador for giving the farewall party in honor of Mr. Moore. It was truly a farewell party. The soldiers, police and correspondents waiting outside heard shots and it was all over. The terrorists surrendered some hours later. A few days after the massacre Mr. William Macomber, the United States Deputy Under Secretary of State, who had been sent to the Sudan to help try to free the hostages, denounced the Black Septembrists as savages and revealed that they had planned to take the American diplomats as hostages to the United States in order to kill them on American soil and the executions had been triggered when the terrorists realized they would not be allowed to get out of the Sudan.

The killings came as an appalling shock to President Sadat, because right up to the moment the triggers were pulled he believed he had been able to duplicate his Bangkok tactic. He had sent an Egyptian plane to Khartoum to bring the Black Septembrists and their hostages to Cairo, and at the time the diplomats were killed Egyptian officials and senior members of Fatah were actually waiting at Cairo for the plane to arrive. The plan was for the Fatah leaders to talk the terrorists into freeing the hostages once the plane had touched down. This situation had come about for a number of reasons. In the first place, Sadat was engaged in a diplomatic campaign designed to win support for Egypt in the "Third World" for his political efforts to force the Israelis to disgorge the land they had swallowed in 1967 and he was fearful that any Arab terrorist action would disrupt that campaign. Secondly, this operation did not have the backing of all the Fatah leadership. It was a wildcat operation by one of the chieftains with Qaddafi's encouragement, and it came at a time when some of the more moderate Fatah leaders were beginning to realize that outright terrorism was counterproductive. Abu Youssef, for instance, the man who was responsible for starting it all with the killing of Wasfi Tell and was also behind the Sabena hijack and the Bangkok affair, later told a friend that he had been opposed to the Khartoum operation because he felt it would damage the Palestinian cause. The fact that Americans were involved also caused a great deal of misgiving among sections of the Fatah leadership. They had no wish to have the full wrath of the United States visited on them—and they were fully justified in this fear.

Sadat made no announcement of his efforts to save the diplomats, but it was noticeable that he did nothing to get the arrested terrorists set free. He had been affronted politically and personally and he does not forgive easily. After all, he was once a terrorist himself, taking part in at least one political assassination, and he knows how these things should be managed.

So, for the first time since the killing of Wasfi Tell, serious doubts about terrorism as a weapon began to be expressed inside Fatah. However, those doubts were not made public and after the killings Black September issued a statement in Beirut in which it vowed to continue its war against "Zionist and American imperialism and their agents in the Arab world." It claimed that the operation had "not at all aimed at bloodshed but had sought the release of our imprisoned heroes" and it mentioned in particular Abu Daoud and Sirhan Sirhan. But, it said, "as a result of the arrogance and the obstinacy of American imperialism, represented by Nixon's statements and by the attitude of hireling tools in Jordan, our revolutionaries carried out the death sentences on three hostages."

It alleged that the three diplomats had "shared in plotting to slaughter our people, conspiring against our Arab nation and our national struggle." It accused Mr. Moore of being "the plotting brain of the American Central Intelligence Agency and one of those directly responsible for the September massacres." It added, "We wish to affirm to the world that the Black September militants have never known fear and will not know it. . . . Its members would not be intimidated by the hypocritical cries of condemnation or the tears of those whom we have never seen shed a tear throughout the quarter of a century during which this [Palestinian] people has been subjected to all kinds of torture and persecution.

"Those who ostensibly weep today over the execution of three enemies of the Arab nation, for which the United States has been directly responsible, realize that thousands of the sons of this people have been atrociously slaughtered and that thousands of others are suffering all kinds of torture in Jordanian and Israeli jails."

The statement ended with the declaration that Black September's "war against Zionist and American imperialism and their agents in the Arab world will continue. Our rifles will remain brandished against both the substance and the shadow."

But these brave words disguised a certain trepidation which quickly turned out to be justified. President Nimeiry's men raided the PLO's office in Khartoum and found a mass of documents linking the organization and Fatah to Black September. This evidence was even more convincing than Abu Daoud's because it could always be argued that his confession had been extracted under torture. But these documents showed that

Fawaz Yassin, the PLO chief in Khartoum, was the "case officer," his deputy, Rizig Abu Gassan, was the leader of the killers and his number three, a Fatah member called Karam, used the PLO's Land-Rover to drive them to the Saudi Embassy. Among the papers were scribbled instructions for the raid and a sketch plan of the embassy and its grounds, as well as the duties assigned to six of the raiding party, each of them under a code name. Karam made a full confession linking Fatah to the raid, and Gassan, who made regular propaganda broadcasts on behalf of Fatah over the Sudanese national radio, told a magistrate's court holding a preliminary hearing into the case: "We are proud of what we have done."

Yassin was in Libya a few days before the attack on the embassy, tying up the details. Then, when the seven Black Septembrists flew in from Beirut to join Rizig Abu Gassan, it was Yassin who met them and saw their luggage through customs. They later admitted having brought in Kalashnikovs, five pistols and eight grenades. Yassin then flew to Libya some hours before the attack, leaving coded instructions for the operation and for the assassination of Emperor Selassie and the West German and British ambassadors. Once Nimeiry's men picked up Yassin's trail Qaddafi was asked to send him back to stand trial, but the Libyan President refused and later helped him to sanctuary in Southern Yemen out of reach of all the people who were after him, the Sudanese, the Israelis, the Americans and those Fatah leaders who recognized the dangers of the Khartoum massacre and would have liked to hand him over as a sacrificial lamb to appease the wrath they knew was about to strike them.

The first result was an angry denunciation of Libya and the Palestinians by Nimeiry, who sent notes to heads of Arab governments accusing Libya of acting in collusion with the terrorists, and the terrorists of having planned operations in the Sudan even more drastic than the killing of the diplomats. He therefore intended, he said, to put an end to the Palestinian organizations' presence in the Sudan.

Qaddafi replied to this attack in typical fashion, accusing the other Arab leaders of having "given up completely the Palestinian cause, and believing that Palestinians are only refugees who can be settled abroad just like companies whose properties are confiscated."

Arafat's reaction was wilder and reflected his fear of American retaliation. Nimeiry, he said, had launched an American-inspired campaign against the guerrillas and he appealed to President Sadat to try to stop this "conspiracy."

But all this merely reflected the internal tensions of Fatah and the Arab world. The real answer to Khartoum came a month later. It was a month in which it was business as usual for the terrorists and the counter-terrorists. The Cypriot ship *Sanya,* on its way to Haifa with 250 Christian pilgrims on board, was badly damaged by a bomb in Beirut harbor. . . . Three cars stuffed with explosives were found in New York when police, acting on an Israeli tip-off, foiled attempts to blow up the El Al office at Kennedy Airport and two Israeli banks in the city. . . . Simha Gilzer was shot in Nicosia. . . . A car bomb destined for the Israeli Embassy in Paris was intercepted by the French police after an Israeli warning. . . . Four suitcases full of explosives and weapons were discovered in passenger lounges at Rome airport. . . . Dr. Kubeisy was shot in Paris. . . . An Arab parcel bomb was discovered in Singapore. . . . Two Arabs carrying Iranian passports were picked up at Rome airport carrying two pistols and six hand grenades. . . . The Israeli Ambassador's home was bombed and the El Al plane attacked in Cyprus.

In the early hours of April 10, 1973, the night after the Cyprus affair, the Israelis struck at the Fatah leadership in the heart of Beirut. It has been suggested that the raid on Beirut was the result of the attacks in Cyprus. But that is not so. The Beirut raid was the result of long-term planning by the Israelis and the first steps in carrying it out had been taken several days before the Cyprus attacks. The Israelis had made a previous attempt to kill Fatah leaders when, on February 21, regular soldiers of the Israeli army landed by helicopter and boat and raided the refugee camps at Baddawi and Nahr el Bared. They hit Nahr el Bared because that is where foreign terrorists—Japanese, Turks, Cypriots and Iranians—are trained. And they crept into Baddawi in the hope of surprising a top-level meeting of guerrilla leaders which their agents had told them was about to take place at the camp. The Israelis went ashore at 8:30 in the evening and laid in wait, but, luckily for the terrorists, the meeting was canceled at the last moment. The Israelis waited until after midnight and then shot up both camps. However, since their raid on Beirut airport in which they destroyed thirteen Arab airliners and caused a great deal of criticism because of their "overkill" tactics, they had carefully limited the scale of their operations in the Lebanese capital. Individual assassinations were judged to be within the limits set by world opinion and American pressure but anything larger was taboo. But then came Khartoum and, backed by the blazing anger of the United States, the Israelis saw the green light for a major operation inside the city.

Six Israeli agents posing as tourists, wearing hippie clothes and carrying false passports, booked into two small but smart hotels near the seafront on April 6 and hired three white Buicks, a Plymouth sedan, a Plymouth station wagon and a Renault from a local auto-rental firm. One of them, posing as an Englishman, stayed at the Coral Beach Hotel, where he told the management that his one passion in life was sea fishing—at night. He went out every night at about midnight and came back a couple of hours later proudly displaying his catch. But on the night of April 9 he did not come back. He had made another catch, the raiding party for which he had been waiting. He guided them into the beach as they landed from fast patrol boats and led them to the six hired cars parked on the promenade. Three of the cars, carrying fifteen men all armed to the teeth with submachine guns and grenades, were driven through the brightly lit nightclub area of Beirut to two apartment blocks just off the Hamra, the city's main shopping center. The raiders attacked three apartments, breaking the doors down, shooting, throwing grenades. The shooting lasted for about ten minutes, and when it was over Abu Youssef, Kamal Adwan and Kamal Nasser, three of the resistance movement's top leaders, lay dead and so did Abu Youssef's wife, who was killed when she threw herself in front of her husband to protect him from the bullets, and a seventy-year-old Italian woman who lived in another of the apartments and, hearing the commotion, looked out her door to see what was happening.

Three of Abu Youssef's bodyguards were also killed in the gunfight that erupted when they challenged the raiding party. A young man we have met before was bady wounded in this gunfight—Ziad Helou, who had taken part in the killing of Wasfi Tell and who had escaped a Jordanian assassination attempt only a week before. It is strange how the theme of Wasfi Tell runs through this story. At the massive memorial service for the dead men held at the Omar Makram mosque in Cairo's Liberation Square, Essat Rabah and Monzer Khalifa, Wasfi Tell's killers, led the procession carrying pictures of the dead Palestinians.

The dead men were prime targets for the Israelis, Abu Youssef in particular. He was ranked Number Three in Fatah behind Yasir Arafat and Abu Iyad and had the killing of Wasfi Tell and the Sabena and Bangkok operations to his credit. It is grimly ironic that at the time of his death he had begun to turn away from terrorism as an effective weapon against the Israelis. Kamal Adwan was in charge of operations in Israeli-occupied territory and Israel proper and was therefore responsible for terrorist attacks which had killed a number of civilians. He fought for his life when the Israelis arrived. His widow, Mrs. Maha Adwan, said she was talking with her husband when they heard shooting and grenades exploding. Five or six men in civilian clothes broke down the door of their apartment just as her husband grabbed his Kalashnikov and opened fire.

"He was able to hit a number of them before he was killed in the doorway of the bedroom," she said. The Israelis announced later that they had lost two dead and two wounded in the night's operations. Kamal Nasser was a different type. He was a bachelor, a Christian and an intellectual who was the official spokesman for the Palestine Liberation Organization. Because of his job and his sophisticated manner he made many friends with Westerners, who were deeply grieved when he was killed. In Tel Aviv I was told by a senior member of the Foreign Service that when the raiders went to his apartment they found two naked girls in his bed, who were asked to dress and leave before Nasser was riddled with bullets. This story enrages Nasser's friends, who say that it is a lie put out by the Israelis to besmirch a good man's name. The truth is very hard to arrive at in this sort of war. There was another tale, that the Israelis were led by a fantastically beautiful girl with long blond hair, which the Israelis will neither confirm nor deny. And there is the persistent story that they were after even bigger game, Yasir Arafat and Abu Iyad, who had attended a long meeting at Nasser's apartment, and that it had been arranged for Arafat to stay with Nasser and for Abu Iyad to stay with Abu Youssef. But, says the story, just as the meeting was breaking up there was a telephone call which led them to leave immediately to drive to Damascus. Later, at Fatah's headquarters in Beirut, I was told that this was not true but that Arafat had taken part in the fighting in one of the commando headquarters also attacked by the Israelis that night. But it was told to me without any corroborating detail and with such a lack of conviction that I deeply suspect its authenticity. The other operations carried out the same night by the Israelis were equally spectacular but did not have the headline appeal of the assassinations. When the raiding force split up, the second group of three cars drove to the main refugee camp of Sabra close to the airport. There they blew up part of the headquarters of Naif Hawatmeh's PDFLP and killed a number of his men in a bloody little battle. They also attacked three other terrorist offices in Beirut, and another diversionary force blew up a terrorist workshop and ammunition cache at Sidon, south of Beirut. When it was all over, after two and a half hours, the raiders took their dead and wounded with them and drove their hired cars back to the promenade, where they parked them neatly in a row—one with bloodstains in its trunk—before being picked up by their boats. The six fake tourists went with them, leaving their baggage behind and their bills unpaid. The manager of one of the hotels complained bitterly: "I started work in this hotel only today and the first thing I had to deal with was police telling me I had Israelis staying in my rooms."

The Israelis were jubilant. Up to this moment they had never officially admitted that they were conducting anti-terrorist operations outside Israel. Now they boasted of their success. General David Elazar told a press conference: "We don't believe that with one operation and one single blow it is possible to stop such [terrorist] activity. But I believe the operation was a severe blow." He went on to warn: "If terrorists can get to Bangkok, Paris, Cyprus, and Rome, their leaders should realize our ability to fight them everywhere." And in the crowded Knesset, Mrs. Golda Meir said, "We killed the murderers who were planning to murder again."

There followed something close to panic among the Palestinians. The fact that the Israelis could waltz into Beirut, kill their leaders and waltz out again was a shattering blow to their morale, for, as the Israelis were quick to point out, this was not a massacre of innocents, a shooting down of pilgrims, or sportsmen or diplomats but an attack on guerrilla leaders who well knew they were involved in a war and well able to defend themselves. Kamal Nasser may have been a "soft target" but Adwan and Abu Youssef were both armed and guarded and the PDFLP headquarters was surrounded by armed commandos.

The first reaction of the Fatah leadership was to broadcast urgent messages to their followers to "scatter and seek shelter," for the Israelis had not only killed, they had also taken with them Kamal Adwan's files on his men who were operating inside Israel and the occupied territories. The files named active Fatah men, local supporters and "sleepers" due to be wakened when the time came. Within days the Israelis mounted a massive round-up of the men and women listed in Adwan's files. Many of them were found to be just names—some of them belonging to people who were dead—used to pad out Adwan's lists. But there were enough genuine names to make Adwan's files a very juicy prize.

The Palestinian leaders took steps to increase their personal safety. A meeting of all the groups belonging to the PLO was called to consider ways of strengthening their security against another attack. More guards were attached to the fedayeen leaders and to the headquarters in the refugee camps. The leaders were told to change their apartments at least once a month and keep their new addresses secret. Their families were evacuated to Syria and Egypt. And they stopped using official PLO vehicles, so that it would be more difficult for their movements to be traced.

At another meeting, of militants this time, plans were discussed for striking back at the Israelis and their "U.S. agents." These proposals included attacks on embassies, the murder of American diplomats, the sabotage of American companies and buildings and the assassination of Arabs known to have co-operated with the American authorities.

For by this time the Arabs had begun to blame the Americans for their disaster in Beirut. Arafat, following up his accusations of an American conspiracy after Khartoum, told a mass meeting at a refugee camp that American involvement had been responsible for the success of the raid and alleged that on the night of the attack a car belonging to the American Embassy had been seen parked near the homes of the three dead leaders and that another car carrying armed men had been seen heading for the embassy. This was indignantly and quite rightly denied by the American Embassy. The Israelis had no help on this operation. Nevertheless, the Arab world continued to blame the United States, if not for active participation, then for supporting the Israelis generally. The Algerian newspaper *La République* said that without the unlimited support of the United States, Israel would not be able to mount such large-scale military operations. In Damascus, the state-owned *Al Thawra* said that the raid "clearly indicates that we are now facing a declared collusion between Israel and the United States. If it was not for the United States and the umbrella it provides for the Israelis, they could not have been able to carry out the murders."

President Richard Nixon ordered a major diplomatic offensive to counter these accusations, and a senior U.S. official said: "We are dealing with an unscrupulous 'Big Lie' situation. It could ignite passions to the point where political murder, wholesale bloodshed and a campaign of mindless vengeance brings war to the Middle East." But Arafat continued his allegations and his threats: "Revenge will come soon," he said, "and it will be terrible." He was obviously referring to the Americans as well as the Israelis. The Voice of Palestine broadcasts all over the Middle East urged "death to the Americans."

The truth of the matter is that after Khartoum the Arabs had convinced themselves that America was certain to work with the Israelis to wipe out Black September and therefore any action undertaken by the Israelis automatically had the Stars and Stripes label pinned on it by the Arabs. The man on whom their suspicions fell was Armin Meyer, the Arabic-speaking former Ambassador to Lebanon who heads the U.S. State Department's Inter-Departmental Working Group on Terrorism. This group was set up in the aftermath of Munich and has a high-powered supreme board consisting of the Secretary of State, the Ambassador to the United Nations and the heads of the CIA and FBI. The Departments involved are Defense; Transportation, which is concerned with hijackings; and the Treasury, which is responsible for the Secret Service, which is itself responsible for the safety of the President. The working group maintains close relations with NATO and CENTO, and Mr. Meyer visits Europe regularly for talks with NATO security officials. It also has bilateral arrangements with several countries. A spokesman for the group says that it has no funds of its own and exists really to coordinate information, consider tactics and set up task forces in cases of emergency. He claimed that good intelligence had enabled it to stifle some terrorist plans but it counts Khartoum as a failure.

The appearance the group tries to give is one of almost passive prevention. But the Arabs look on it differently. Bassam Abu Sherif, the PFLP spokesman, was vehement about Mr. Meyer and his work. Abu Sherif insisted to me that Meyer's group had established an operations room in Beirut which was staffed by some of America's leading intelligence experts and that the American anti-terrorist plan was drawn up under three headings: (1) the protection of United States personnel, (2) the protection of oil companies and installations and (3) the liquidation of "international terrorism"—he said that meant the Palestinians—because of its potential threat to U.S. interests. Abu Sherif also said that a common body had been set up by Jordan, Israel and the United States to pool their information on Arab terrorism. Jordan, he said, had been given charge of maintaining security in several Gulf oil states and Israel had been given a free hand to operate against Arabs in Europe, despite the objections of the British government, which tried to convince the Americans that the European countries ought to look after their own security and that to give the Israelis carte blanche was an invitation to more bloodshed.

Certainly, after Khartoum there appeared to be an increase in the exchange of information between the Israelis and the Americans, and the Israelis seemed to be on a freer rein in their counter-terrorism activities, while the CIA stepped up its own efforts to infiltrate the terrorist organizations. This was naturally difficult for Americans born in the United States because of the rigorous security checks imposed by the guerrillas and so the Americans were forced to use local agents, not always with the best results. Those that did manage to infiltrate acquired only low-grade information and several were killed when their covers slipped. So although the Americans may provide facilities and support and pass on information gathered all over the world, the real intelligence work on Black September and PFLP is done by the Israelis and they are brilliant at it. They must have at least one man very near the top of the Palestinian hierarchy.

When the raiders went ashore at Beirut, they knew precisely who they were after and they knew exactly which doorbells to ring. In an attack across the Lebanese border on a Fatah village, a silent figure, his face masked in a Balaclava helmet, sat in a half-track and pointed out specific houses to the Israeli soldiers. Every one was a bull's-eye, containing Fatah commanders or offices. Who was he? "Our Fatah man," said the Israeli commander. They missed the commando leaders at the Baddawi camp only because the top-secret meeting was called off at the last moment. Before this raid the Palestinian officer in charge of the camp's security was called on his personal telephone and told not to worry if he heard helicopters approaching. They would, he was informed, be Lebanese army helicopters on exercise. The helicopters duly arrived. But they were Israeli, not Lebanaese. One security man said later that "such detailed knowledge could only have come from someone constantly living inside the camps and it must have been more than one individual, there must have been someone accepted by the commando leaders and someone able to get the information out quickly." Confirmation of the accuracy of the Israelis' information came with the finding of a map dropped by an Israeli officer. It was an aerial photograph of the camp on which all the targets were ringed. It was accurate and up to date.

On August 10, 1973, Dr. George Habash was waiting at Beirut airport to catch an Iraqi Caravelle when his suspect heart started to cause him pain. Unwilling to risk another heart attack, he canceled his flight. The Caravelle took off at 9:45 P.M. without him and a few minutes later it was intercepted by Israeli fighters and escorted to a military airport in northern Israel, where it was forced to land and troops stormed aboard searching for Habash. When it was discovered that he was not on the plane it was allowed to resume its flight to Iraq. There was of course a great deal of international criticism of the Israelis.

Sir Donald Maitland, Britain's delegate to the United Nations, told the Security Council that Israel had committed an "act of official violence" which in no circumstances could be justified. "My Government," he said, "cannot accept that any government is entitled to take the law into its own hands and itself commit acts of violence totally inconsistent with international law." France and China took an equally strong line and even the United States, Israel's supporter, joined the fifteen-nation Council in unanimously condemning Israel, saying it deplored: "this violation of Lebanese sovereignty and the United Nations charter and the rule of law in civil aviation." But the Israelis were so anxious to capture Habash they were prepared to accept the condemnation gladly. They would pay almost any price to get their hands on the man whose organization has been responsible for so much bloodshed and who still remains the grand master of this most dedicated group of modern assassins.

From the intelligence point of view, the hijacking showed intimate knowledge of the movements of one of the most closely guarded and secretive of the Palestinian leaders. Such knowledge could only have come from someone very close to Habash. Only his bad heart made that knowledge useless at the last moment.

The Palestinian organizations have in fact been penetrated through and through by the Israelis and the Jordanians—King Hussein's intelligence service is estimated to have three-hundred men working in Beirut—at various levels. But the super-spy, the man at the top, must be an extremely brave and resourceful character. The fedayeen security checks are stringent and each time the Israelis carry out a coup there is a flurry of anti-spy activity throughout the various groups. So if the super-spy is an Israeli he must have a perfect cover and eat, drink, sleep and think not only like an Arab but like an Arab terrorist, and if he is an Arab turned traitor he must consider every movement he makes, every word he says. In either case a dreadful death awaits him if he is caught.

The knowledge that the Israelis had such a man and many others inside the commando movement was one of the most demoralizing results of the Beirut assassinations. The bright possibilities shown by the killing of Wasfi Tell and the high point of Munich seemed a long way away. Now they were beleaguered, attacked in their own camps, killed in their homes in the center of Beirut and hunted through Europe. Their men were arrested in Israel, there was opposition mounting in their own ranks to the use of terror and they were sure that the security forces of America and Israel had united to wipe them out. All these factors combined to send their morale plummeting.

They were also under attack from another direction—from the Lebanese, their unwilling hosts. Throughout 1972 and the early part of 1973 the Israeli army and air force had been making regular forays across the Lebanese border to strike at the guerrilla bases in "Fatahland," the wild and desolate area in southern Lebanon which had been given to the commandos for their training ground and for mounting their rocket attacks and border infiltrations. The Israeli raids grew heavier with armored task forces roaming the Lebanese countryside, and with the raids went increasingly severe warnings to the Lebanese government to curb the guerrillas' activities—or else. This the Lebanese did, interposing their army between the Israelis and the Palestinians who filtered back to the refugee camp headquarters bitter about what they considered their betrayal by the Lebanase. This feeling festered in the aftermath of the Beirut raid, with the fedayeen complaining that the Lebanese army had not given them sufficient protection and even suggesting that the army had conspired with the Israelis in an effort to wipe out their leadership. Certainly there was no love lost between the army and the "feds." The regular soldiers, only fourteen thousand strong, looked with envy on the splendid weapons supplied to the guerrillas by Russia, and they feared the growing strength of the commandos who were their equal in number and had turned their refugee camps into armed fortresses bristling with machine guns, rockets and even antiaircraft guns. Tension grew until Beirut, for all its noisy gaiety and lush living, began to have a touch of the smell of Amman in September 1970 about it. As usual in these situations, the explosion was sparked by a small incident, the arrest by Naif Hawatmeh's men of three Lebanese soldiers.

The army went in to get their men and general fighting broke out between the guerrillas and the soldiers. After a few days a sort of peace was patched up, but it lasted only long enough for guerrillas in a speeding car to chuck a bomb at an army officers' club alongside the lush Phoenicia Hotel. This time the fighting became really serious. Saiqa commandos infiltrated from Syria to bolster the fedayeen fighting in the refugee camps. Rockets were fired into the grounds of the Presidential Palace. Armored cars hammered the refugee camps with cannon fire. The Prime Minister resigned. Civil war threatened. The Israelis massed on the border. There was a flurry of delegates from other Arab countries who tried to work out a settlement. Casualties mounted and before the fighting was over some four hundred people had died. The areas around the guerrilla camps were wrecked, with smoke-blackened holes from cannon shells and smaller pits dug by machine-gun bullets marking the sides of modern blocks of apartments.

President Suleiman Frangie eventually brought the fighting under control by sending in his British-built Hawker Hunters to strafe the refugee camps. This shocked the guerrillas, who never imagined that the peaceful Lebanese would employ such Israeli-type tactics against them. However, Frangie was forced to restrain his army by the pressure of the other Arab states, who were desperate to avoid another "Black September." Frangie arranged a cease-fire with Arafat, and Lebanon, although unhappily counting the cost in casualties and the loss of a summer's earnings from the tourist trade, gradually returned to its normal state of frenzy.

But for the fedayeen there could be no return to normal. They had lost many of their best fighting men, the militants who provided the manpower for Black September's operations.

It was months before the terrorists were able to resume large-scale operations.

The lull in terrorist activity was most noticeable in Europe and the reason was that among the papers the Israelis had seized in Kamal Adwan's apartment were details of prospective operations in Europe and lists of Fatah agents and European sympathizers. The terrorist leaders were not sure of the extent of the information captured by the Israelis, and so they were forced to remake the whole of their European organization, replacing agents, changing codes and abandoning missions that were ready to be carried out. This organization was extensive, based on Arab embassies and representatives of Arab organizations that seemed to have no connection with terrorism. These men were the "agents in place," the local organizers who arranged things for the action groups. It was Munich which demonstrated the extent of the Arab infrastructure inside Europe. Seemingly innocent men were proved to be up to their necks in clandestine work. One of them was Abdullah al Franji, an official at the Arab League's office in Bonn. His telephone number was among the papers found on one of the dead terrorists on Furstenfeldbruck airfield. He was tipped off and skipped out of Germany just before the police arrived with a deportation order. When they searched his apartment they found five walkie-talkies which had been converted to transmit high-frequency signals designed to detonate bombs planted up to a mile away. There was a certain inevitability in Black September's choice of Germany for its first major exercise in holding the world to ransom, for Fatah was founded in Germany, at the University of Stuttgart, in the 1950s. Many young Palestinians went to Germany to study after the Arab defeat of 1948, and among those studying at Stuttgart were Yasir Arafat, Hani al Hassan and Khalil al Wazir. Arafat, supported by his two friends, soon established himself as an uncompromising nationalist. He gathered around him Arabs of a like mind who were studying not only in Stuttgart but in other universities in Germany and Austria, and founded Fatah, dedicated to the liberation of Palestine from the Israelis.

By the early sixties Fatah was the most powerful political organization among the Palestinian students, and Arafat and Khalil al Wazir moved on to spread its gospel in the Middle East, leaving Hani al Hassan to run Germany and Austria. Arafat, as we have seen, came into his own after the Six Day War and Khalil al Wazir remained by his side, one of the leading figures in Fatah and, under the code name of Abu Jihad, one of the chieftains of Black September.

Fatah's influence in Germany remained strong, and at the time of Munich there were some 4,000 Arabs studying there and another 37,000 Arabs at work in Germany's factories. The workers, being paid by German industry, and the students, supported by German scholarships, were making regular monthly subscriptions to the Palestinian war chest. However, after Munich, the Germans expelled about a hundred of the more militant Arabs and disbanded the General Union of Palestinian Students and the General Union of Palestinian Workers. It was emphasized that the aim of the ban on these "radical organizations" was not to prevent them from pursuing their political objectives but to preserve Germans and peaceful foreigners living in Germany from terrorism. There was a great outcry in the Arab states about this "inhumane treatment of innocent workers and students." But the expulsions and bannings seemed to have little effect on the activities of the Palestinians, who simply moved over the border into East Germany and carried on with their work. By the late summer of 1973 clandestine activity began to build up again in West Germany and the feeling was that it was being directed from East Germany. This was the first time that the Communist states had become actively involved in terrorism and it was an indication of a change in direction that was taking place among the terrorists, who were swinging away from Fatah's limited aim of liberating Palestine to PFLP's philosophy of world revolution.

8 • The Danger in Europe

ANOTHER INDICATION OF THE support Arab terrorism was getting from the apostles of world revolution came at the trial in West Berlin of Horst Mahler, a lawyer who was accused of founding the Baader-Meinhof gang of urban guerrillas. There was loud applause from his supporters in court when he praised "the bravery" of the Munich killers. The Germans have special problems in dealing with the Arabs and one official involved in the anti-terrorist program believes that Germany "is the most favorable country for all Black September-type operations" because of the German political and moral complexes following the Hitler regime and its racial policies. "Our complex about Hitler and the Jews has become overlaid by the Socialism and the Arabs syndrome." The German authorities, he says, are therefore easily blackmailed by foreign terrorists with a "moral" cause.

The rest of Europe does not have this uniquely German problem, but the terrorist setup revealed by the investigations after Munich is common to most European countries. There is no point in trying to pretend that one can present a neat blueprint showing a chain of command and regional or national groupings. Nobody can. For it does not exist as a permanent entity. Black September in Europe as seen by Western intelligence resembles a basketful of vipers with more tails than heads and even when an occasional head is pulled out it often does not belong to the tail that was being watched. Constant flux, stemming from shifts of loyalties and quarrels between groups or from the desertion, disillusionment, arrest or death of key individuals, is the characteristic of Arab terrorism in Europe. Nevertheless, the over-all picture is constant and this is the way that picture looks country by country:

Switzerland

Daoud Barakat, a thirty-one-year-old Palestinian from Jerusalem who has held both Algerian and Jordanian papers, works in Geneva officially as a representative of the Democratic Yemeni Republic at the United Nations headquarters, but he seems to spend more time dealing with Palestinian affairs than either Yemen's or the United Nations'.

It was he who flew home to Beirut with the body of the dead terrorist-philosopher Fuad Shemali when Shemali died of cancer in Geneva. The Israelis say that he is the head of Black September for the whole of Europe. Barakat vehemently denies this accusation: "I reject these allegations absolutely. They make me laugh." But the Israelis are in no doubt about his connections with Black September. They accuse him of being one of the planners of Munich and because of this he figures on the Wrath of God's death list.

The importance of Geneva to Black September is that it is an operational transit point for fedayeen traveling from the

Middle East to assignments in Europe. Passports, money, arms and communications are available and few points in Europe are more than a couple of hours' flying time away.

Italy

The importance of Rome is that the Black September organization there is based on the original Razd setup and is probably the best entrenched and most secure of all the European branches. The Italian authorities believe that the city is the contact point for European operations where "agents in place" can go to receive their orders and where strategy-planning talks are held in a number of apartments. Weapons are stored there too, in the cellars of what the Italian security people describe as "the embassy of one particular Arab nation which is committed to a total 'Holy War' against Israel." The reference is obvious: the Libyan Embassy. For its manpower, Black September draws on the 2,000 Arab students at the universities of Rome and Perugia. Another reason why Rome is so important is that its chaotic international airport provides a vital aerial crossroads. Practically every airliner going anywhere touches down at Rome and the opportunities for hijacking and mayhem are rich. It was from Rome that the "kamikazes" of Lod set out. It was there that that the two English girls were given the exploding tape recorder. At one time Rome was a byword for lax airport security. But after Lod it tightened considerably. In April 1973 two Arabs carrying forged Iranian passports were caught carrying two pistols each and with six hand grenades tied around their waists in special belts. In another incident an attractive young Lebanese girl trying to board an airliner was found to have two pistols strapped to her inner thighs.

One of the great problems of all the European officials who arrest terrorists is, of course, what to do with them. These arrests so often lead to further outrages carried out to secure the release of the prisoners that the attitude of many countries is:

Why should we hold prisoners if their presence is going to mean the death of innocent people? Italy wants no trouble with Black September, and although Dr. Bonaventura Provenza, the burly Sicilian head of Rome's "Political Office" who is in charge of anti-terrorism, says: "As far as we are concerned all Arabs who set foot on Italian soil are automatically regarded as possible Black September terrorists," the fact remains that few terrorists stay long in Italian prisons.

There was a great outcry in August 1973 when the prisons were cleared of terrorists, with four of them being released in forty-eight hours. Two of them were the "Iranians" caught carrying weapons at the airport. They had been sentenced to four years but served only four months. The other two were Hamit Abdul Shibli, a Jordanian, and Abdel Hadi Nakaa, a Syrian, who had been arrested in June when the Mercedes they were driving through the center of Rome blew up. It was found to be loaded with automatic weapons and plastic explosives.

Critics of the Italian government complained that it was releasing potential killers at the same time as it was prosecuting village grocers for raising food prices. But there is no doubt that this criticism carried little weight against the fact that the Italian oil industry is completely at the mercy of the Arabs.

France

The terrorist organization in Paris is based largely on the thousands of Algerians and Moroccans who study and work in the city, and on the radical left-wing intelligentsia, which supported the Algerians in their war against the French army and which now supports the Palestinians. During the riots of 1968 which brought about President de Gaulle's retirement, many of the younger, more militant left-wingers believed that they were on the verge of creating a new revolution in France. They failed largely because the people they thought would join them, the workers, wanted nothing to do with revolution, and when it was all over and their movement began to splinter and lose its effectiveness, the police were quick to jump on any hint of urban terror. So some of them turned to the Arab terrorist movements for fulfillment. The Arabs held a double fascination: first there was the thrill of violence, of taking part in a revolution, and then there was the Rudolph Valentino "Sheik on a White Steed" type of sexual attraction that Arabs seem to exercise over a certain type of European woman.

One woman who got caught up ideologically in the terrorist cause was an attractive twenty-five-year-old blonde, a teacher of English in the Paris suburbs who also worked as a cashier at the avant-garde théâtre de l'Ouest, which was sponsored by the French government and whose manager was none other than Mohammed Boudia, the man the Israelis claim was Black September's boss in France and whom they blew to pieces with a car bomb in the Rue des Fosses-St.-Bernard.

People like Evelyne were of great importance to the terrorists. Ideologically committed, good-looking, she could go where Arabs could not. Her first mission was to blow up the Gulf oil installations at Rotterdam. She spent a week in the city planning the operation with an Algerian, returned to Paris to report and then with a Frenchman and a Palestinian drove back to Holland, cut through the protective fence around the oil tanks, positioned their delayed-action bombs and then drove off. They were across the French border at midnight when their 150 kilos of "plastique" went up in three explosions which could be heard in The Hague. Evelyne's group in Paris included Nadia and Marlene Bardali, daughters of a rich merchant of Casablanca who were more lovesick than ideologically committed, and it was they who brought about Evelyne's downfall. The three women, along with an elderly French couple who had been given £850 and round-trip air tickets to smuggle detonators and timing devices into Israel, formed what was called "The Easter Commando." The plan was for them to blow up nine tourist hotels in Israel during the crowded Easter ceremonies of 1971. But the Israeli police picked up the mini-skirted sisters and they quickly told everything they knew, leading the Israelis to Evelyne and the French couple. To their considerable astonishment the Israelis found that the three girls were walking bombs. They had explosives concealed in the false lining of their brassieres and girdles, in their lipsticks and Tampax and in the hollowed heels of their shoes. The linings of the Moroccan girls' long, modish coats were impregnated with an explosive liquid, while Evelyne carried another chemical which, when combined with the inflammable material of the coats, created a napalm effect. The sisters told the court that they had acted out of love for their Arab boy friends, and they were described in some Lebanese newspapers as the "nymphomaniac terrorists." Evelyne was made of sterner stuff. She told the court: "I considered the Palestinians' cause against Israel the same as that created by French colonization in Algeria. That's why I wanted to help them." However, after she had been sentenced to fourteen years' imprisonment, she said: "I have been an instrument and I hope my sentence will be a warning to young girls who might also be swept up."

She also provided the Israelis with a list of names and addresses in France, including that of the makeshift laboratory where her explosives were made. The labs were raided, but the Algerian explosives experts who worked there had already flown.

One of the Israelis' complaints about the way European countries treat Arab terrorists is that the French in particular are dilatory in acting on Israeli tip-offs on terrorist activity. The French in their turn complain that the Israelis send them such long lists of names of suspected terrorists that they could not possibly investigate let alone arrest them all.

Austria

Terrorist activity in Austria has been closely linked with the German organization ever since the establishment of Fatah, but from 1971, when the Russian authorities started to allow large numbers of Russian Jews to emigrate to Israel, there was one prime target in Austria—Schonau Castle, the transit camp through which most of the 70,000 Jews allowed out by the Russians have passed on the way to their Promised Land. The Arabs always argued that Schonau was a legitimate target because the young men who passed through there would soon be in the Israeli army, fighting against the Arabs. The Israelis therefore kept a very close watch on the castle and the Black September organization in Austria. They were able to warn the Austrian police on more than one occasion in time to foil attacks on the castle, and in one incident in January 1973 the Austrians arrested three Palestinians who had been "fingered" by the Israelis. Their interrogation revealed that another group of three planned to join them, and this second group was arrested as they crossed the border from Italy. They all admitted to being members of Black September on a European mission. They had set out from Beirut and had exchanged the Syrian passports they were carrying for false Israeli papers in Geneva before moving on to Austria. Their plan was to enter Schonau posing as Israelis, occupy it and then blow it up. Schonau remained safe until September 28, 1973, when two Palestinians, Mustafa Soudeidan and Mahmoud Khaldo, who said they were members of a group called "The Eagles of the Palestinian Revolution,"* came across the Czechoslovakian border, produced pistols and hand grenades and took an Austrian customs official and three newly arrived Jews hostage. A curious aspect of this affair is that both these men had been turned back three weeks before by Austrian border officials who recognized that their documents were forged. The fact that they were allowed a second attempt from Czechoslovakia, a country which does not lack diligence in its examination of passports, argues that there was official Czechoslovakian connivance in the incident. The

---

*They were later proved to be members of the Syrian-controlled El Saiga, who hid their true identity in order not to embarrass the Syrian government.

Austrians had no chance to send them back a second time. They produced their pistols with their papers, seized their hostages and delivered their ultimatum: The Austrian government must close down Schonau or they would kill the hostages. They held grenades with the safety pins clenched between their teeth to prove their point, and in the now customary fashion they had leaflets written in English justifying their action as a "retaliation for Zionist crimes."

After fourteen hours of negotiation Chancellor Bruno Kreisky, himself a Jew, surrendered unconditionally. He gave his word to the terrorists that Schonau would be closed in return for the lives of the hostages. Later, he was to reply to criticism by asking the critics: "Have you ever had to make a decision literally involving life or death?" But the criticism was intense. The Israelis were enraged, and in an emotional speech Mrs. Meir told a hushed assembly of the Council of Europe in Strasbourg: "This is a great victory for terrorist organizations. This is the first time a government has come to an agreement of this kind." She said that the Vienna affair was at the very heart of the Arab-Israeli conflict because, although the State of Israel had existed for twenty-five years, it had never enjoyed a single full year of peace. "Israel is not a people of angels but of men and women wishing to live decently. Israel wanted to live in peace but others were resorting to terrorism because they had lost the war. The Arab terrorist organizations, helped by their governments, are carrying out terrorism and violence in Europe. Terrorism has to be wiped out; there can be no deals with terrorists. The terrible fact of Vienna is that a deal, an agreement, an understanding—I'm trying to use the kindest words—was made. I'm convinced that what has happened is the greatest encouragement to terrorism throughout the world. . . ."

Mrs. Meir went from Strasbourg to Vienna to try to persuade Chancellor Kreisky to change his mind, arguing that there was no validity in concessions extracted under threat of murder.

But Kreisky would not budge, influenced no doubt by the terrorist mouthpiece in Beirut, *Al Moharrer,* which carried a threat from the Eagles of the Palestine Revolution that "it would not serve Austria's stability and interests or contribute to the safety of its citizens" if Kreisky changed his mind. There was also widespread suspicion that Kreisky was not too unhappy to shut down Schonau, as such a prime target on Austrian soil was a considerable embarrassment to a country which has of necessity taken great care to remain neutral in all things since World War II. The *Sunday Telegraph* of London summed up its feelings about Kreisky's behavior with the one-word headline: CRAVEN.

There were some interesting sidelights to the Schonau affair: Chancellor Kreisky, who describes himself as "an agnostic of Jewish birth," has a brother, Paul, who lives in Israel. . . . The Eagles of the Palestine Revolution later revealed themselves as members of the Syrian-supported Saiqa organization and said that they had adopted the pseudonym in order not to embarrass the Syrian government but that once the War of the Day of Antonement had started they felt able to announce their true identity. . . . Two psychiatrists, Professor Friedrich Hacker and Dr. Willibald Sluga, who were sent by the Austrian government to talk to the two terrorists through the window of the Volkswagen bus they had commandeered and to make recommendations on how best to handle the situation, later reported that both the terrorists were probably under the influence of drugs. The report said: "They felt subject to the pressure, real or imagined, of their superiors' commands and typified the professional terrorist personality; fanatical, well trained and thoroughly prepared for this particular mission. Thoroughly indoctrinated by stereotyped propaganda, they clung firmly to their paranoic belief in their own power and their ecstatically heightened fantasies of aggression directed against both themselves and others." The psychiatrists described the terrorists as "fanatically indoctrinated, determined to go to any lengths, perfectly capable of recognizing any delaying tactics, and constantly threatening to bring the affair to a bloody conclusion." The report added that the drugs it was believed the terrorists were using led to an overestimation of their users' own value and to risks being underestimated or disregarded. The threat of bloodshed was consequently increased by the probable effect of the drugs, which, particularly as their effect were off, were known to lead to irrational, unforeseeable reactions. The Israelis argue that this report could well justify making some sort of deal with the terrorists at the time but they continue to insist that no agreement under the threat of death is valid. This affair would have been the cause of much international trouble if it had not been wiped off the front pages by the outbreak of war on October 6, 1973.

Great Britain

The authorities in Britain have tended to regard Black September as, according to one member of the Special Branch, "potentially a big threat but practically a small problem." There are two main reasons for this confidence: (1) Britain is an island with particularly severe passport and immigration controls aimed at preventing illegal immigration. This is in contrast to the Continent, where there is such ease of movement across the borders and only perfunctory passport control. An identity card is all that is required to pass from one Common Market country to another on the mainland of Europe. (2) There is no large indigenous Arab population to give camouflage to the terrorists as there is in Germany with its workers and students and France with its large North African community. A third factor which might be added is the inherent respect the Arabs have for the British police, their opponents on many occasions in the Middle East when Britain was the dominant power there.

Arab terrorist activity in Britain is further curtailed by the fact that the British police keep a very close watch on anybody who might have terrorist sympathies, not only because of the threat posed by Black September but because of the bomb attacks carried out by the IRA. They are extremely interested in IRA links with Black September. Ali Hassan Salameh is known to have made contact with Seamus Costello, Adjutant General of the IRA, and at one stage it was feared that cooperation between thse two organizations might jell into action, but these fears have so far proved groundless, just as the bright hopes of George Habash's terrorist international have faded.

Nevertheless, the "Sheik on a White Steed" syndrome is prevalent among British women and the "Lawrence of Arabia" syndrome among British men. The symptom of both these syndromes is a blind belief that all Arabs are romantic, courteous Bedouins leading a peaceful, nomadic existence in the desert. There is also a great deal of genuine distress in Britain about the conditions in the refugee camps, and Britons like Dr. Diane Campbell-Lefevre who have worked in these camps come to support the Arab contention that life in the camps not only explains but justifies terrorism. But if one points out that if the Arab nations had spent just a fraction of what they have spent on arms to resettle the refugees, the answer one gets is: Why should the Arabs do the Israelis' work for them and wipe out the few remaining centers where the idea of a Palestinian nation can be maintained? This type of support for Black September was expressed two weeks after Munich by Mr. Louis Eaks, a former chairman of the Young Liberals. Opposing a motion put at a Young Liberal conference which condemned "those who used kidnapping and piracy to enforce their wishes," he said: "Munich had to happen" to make people open their eyes to the plight of the Palestinians and "if you lived for twenty-four years in a Palestinian refugee camp you might find yourselves on the next plane to Munich or Amsterdam or somewhere else." Britain also has a number of influential and vocal supporters of the Arab cause, including Members of Parliament, who, although never publicly approving of terrorism, also never raise their voices to condemn it, thereby approving of it by silence. However, there are an equal number of influential Britons who do condemn the terrorists and they have successfully opposed the setting up of a PLO office in London and also a projected visit to Britain by Yasir Arafat.

Britain has only once been faced with a hostage situation, and that was when Captain Uri Bar-Lev brought the captured hijacker Leila Khaled into Heathrow airport. She was the center of a two-way struggle. The Israelis wanted her deported to Tel Aviv to stand trial and the Arabs wanted her released. The Arabs, with more than four hundred hostages at Dawson's Field, obviously had the weightier case and she was flown out to Beirut. The Israelis did not like it but the whole affair became lost in the drama of the events taking place in Jordan.

For a time Britain was the only European country to have a Black Septembrist under sentence. He was Mohammed Abdul Karin Fuheid, a twenty-four-year-old Palestinian who described himself as a lieutenant in Fatah and was arrested when attempting to pass through London airport carrying weapons and explosives for use in an attack on the Israeli Embassy in Stockholm. He was booked through to Sweden and as he was in transit his baggage would not normally have been inspected at Heathrow, merely transferred from one plane to another. But he had the misfortune to arrive on Christmas Eve 1972 and the porters were more concerned with their Christmas cheer than carrying passengers' baggage, so Fuheid had to carry his own bags and pass through customs, where the arms were found and he was arrested. He was charged with being in illegal possession of a Browning automatic pistol and fifty-one rounds of ammunition and sentenced to eighteen months' imprisonment at the Old Bailey. Because he was potentially a man for whom hostages would be seized, extraordinary precautions were taken, especially in Malta and Cyprus, to guard British personnel and aircraft. But it seems that the sentence was too light and Fuheid too small a nish for Black September to mount an operation to free him. He earned full remission on his sentence and has been released. In another incident at Heathrow, on May 21, 1973, the British police, acting on an Israeli tip-off that an Arab was likely to leave Britain to take part in an operation in Europe, arrested two Arabs as they were about to board a plane. They were questioned by Scotland Yard detectives, but the information obtained was said in British police terms to be "insufficient to justify the institution of criminal proceedings." The Arabs were deported. Other incidents on British soil were the killing of Dr. Shachori, the attempted assassination of Ambassador Rifai and, in 1969, bomb explosions at the Israeli ZIM shipping line offices and the Oxford Street branch of Marks and Spencer, the Jewish-owned chain store where most of the Arab visitors to London do their shopping. They were all treated with a great display of imperturbability, but then came two incidents which shattered the calm. On December 30, 1973, a man knocked at the door of the president of Marks and Spencer, Mr. Joseph "Teddy" Sieff, in Queens Grove, St. John's Wood, shortly before 7 P.M. The butler, Manuel Terloria, opened the door and was confronted by a young man wearing a parka with its hood pulled over his head and with his face covered to the nose by a dark woollen material who pointed a 9-mm. automatic at the butler and ordered him inside and demanded to be taken to Mr. Sieff. Terloria led the gunman into the lounge, which was empty, and was then ordered upstairs. At the top of the stairs on the second floor is a bathroom and Mr. Sieff was inside when the door was thrown open and the gunman fired at him with the gun less than three feet from his head. A few seconds before this happened, Mr. Sieff's wife, Lois, had come out of the bedroom at the other end of the landing and saw the butler being shoved forward with the gun at his back. She ran back to her bedroom and dialed 999 for the police. She was telling them what she had seen when she heard a shot. Her husband, who is rich and a devoted supporter of Israel, is also extremely lucky. The bullet had gone into his upper jaw, dead center beneath his nose. It had missed his jugular vein by a hairbreadth and come to rest at the back of his head. There is little doubt that his wife's emergency call saved his life, and almost had the gunman captured. The first police car arrived on the secene only ninety seconds after the gunman had fled and an ambulance came quickly afterward and rushed the wounded man to a hospital. He made an extraordinary recovery and praised his strong teeth for knocking the power out of the bullet. But the gunman disappeared. No one knows who he was, and, although PFLP immediately claimed credit for the affair, the British police still have no leads in the case whatsoever. They have, however, tightened the security watch they keep on prominent British Jews.

The other incident came just a week later when troops in tanks and armored cars joined forces with the police in sealing off five square miles around Heathrow International Airport. Armored personnel carriers were stationed under the flight path of incoming aircraft. Cars were stopped and searched. Armored vehicles could be seen all over the airport. And machine-gun posts were set up by unusually serious troops. In strike-plagued Britain this extremely unusual joint exercise between the police and the army was condemned by the left wing as a try-out of a plan to use troops "in aid of the civil power" against militant workers on strike and there was wild talk about a military dictatorship being planned. But that was not what the panic at Heathrow was about. It was about SAM 7 antiaircraft missiles. It was known that the terrorists had acquired a batch of these missiles (I will tell how later) and the authorities had been tipped off that, smuggled into Britain in the diplomatic bag by sympathetic Arab embassies, they would be used to shoot down an El Al airliner taking off or landing at Heathrow. It may be that the operation was mounted in such a massive and blatant fashion in order to scare off the would-be rocketeers, but a modified form of the military watch on Heathrow has been maintained ever since. No chances are being taken.

The man on whom Palestinian resistance activity in Britain centers is Said Hammani, the PLO's representative, who, although he has not been allowed to open his own office, has a room at the Arab League offices in Hay Hill, Mayfair. He is given Specal Branch protection—not only to protect him but also to keep an eye on his movements. Hammani, like all official PLO and Fatah representatives abroad, denies all connection with Black September. Interviewed in London, he said: "Politically we are against Black September. We don't agree with the tactics." But then he went on to make the common qualification: "But I understand this Black September. I understand why they have turned to terrorism." This is the official Fatah line on Black September. Arafat follows it, so does Abu Iyad and so does Daoud Barakat.

Hammani made no bones about his feelings for the Israelis: "My father and mother were forced to leave Jaffa. Haganah came to Jaffa when the British withdrew and they ordered us to leave our homes through loud-hailers mounted on lorries: 'You have fifteen minutes to leave before the house is demolished.'"

Sitting in his bare office with its locked front door and spy hole he talked about the death threats he received: "Of course they want me dead. I ignore all these threats because I have to accept the risk as part of my duty."

He added: "I think there is no way out of this terrorism. I think it will expand. I don't blame them. I don't accept their methods. We condemn everything Black September has done. But we understand it. We are not criminals, but we have a duty to fight for our homeland and we must fight. Black September came to London once, so they can come again. I don't know if they are here." The telephone rang. He picked it up and joked: "Maybe we will now hear news about Black September." It is only right to point out that Hammani, while denying any association with Black September, is automatically, as the PLO's representative, also the representative of the PFLP, and there is no doubt about that organization's terrorist activities.

There is also no doubt about the international spread of terrorism, and much of this spread is carried out by diplomatic means. Mr. Philip Goodhart, the Conservative Member of Parliament for Beckenham, claimed to have evidence which he passed to MI 5 that the submachine gun used in the attempt on Ambassador Rifai's life was brought to England in a diplomatic bag. In Holland in October 1972 an Arab traveling on diplomatic papers was caught at the Amsterdam airport with two suitcases containing hand grenades, pistols and some forty unaddressed letter bombs. He was described as "R.H. a thirty-three-year-old Palestinian traveling on an Algerian diplomatic passport from Damascus and attached to an Algerian embassy in South America." He was held for twenty-four hours and then released to continue his journey to South America, because, the police said, they could not prove that he knew what was in the suitcases. He claimed he had been given them just before he left Damascus. A likely story! That same month Mr. Asher Ben Nathan, the forthright Israeli Ambassador to France, told members of the Anglo-American Press Association in Paris that "the kind of terrorism that took place at Munich would not be possible without the complicity of the diplomatic pouch." Even with road travel, he said, "it is easy to pass frontiers with a crate of machine guns if your car has diplomatic plates."

The Algerian and Libyan embassies are believed to be the worst offenders against diplomatic tradition. It is, of course, a very simple matter for a terrorist to arrive "clean" in a country, then go to an embassy to pick up weapons brought into the country in the diplomatic bag.

9 • Death and Dissension

B<small>Y THE AUTUMN OF</small> 1973 the terrorists had
begun to try to demonstrate that they had recovered from the
effects of the Beirut raid. They revamped their organizations,
substituted new codes and went into action again. The Schonau
affair was one of these resurgent operations. Another was the
hijacking of a Japan Air Lines Jumbo jet with 123 passengers
on board thirty minutes after it left Amsterdam on July 20
bound for Tokyo via Anchorage, Alaska. It turned south and
as it passed Cyprus the skyjackers broadcast a message through
Nicosia's control tower which said: "We are determined to
fight imperialism unto death." But the operation was already a
failure, because its leader, a girl, was dead, killed by her own
grenade. She was sipping champagne in the Jumbo's cocktail
bar soon after the airliner left Amsterdam when the grenade
she was carrying strapped to her waist exploded, killing her,

wounding a steward and precipitating seizure of the airliner. She was a mystery woman; no details were given about her, although some reports said that she was a Christian Iraqi who had succeeded Leila Khaled as the leading PFLP woman terrorist. Her fellow terrorists, who included Arabs, Japanese and one European, called themselves "The Sons of the Occupied Territory," a completely new name in the Palestinian Who's Who, and it is believed that they were another breakaway PFLP group, with the Japanese being colleagues of Kozo Okamoto in the Red Army.

They were lost without their leader, for only she knew the objective of the mission and where to take the plane. After an initial demand for the release of Kozo Okamoto, they made no more ultimatums but hunted desperately around the Middle East for a safe haven. Beirut turned them away, so did Basra and Bahrein. Eventually they landed in Dubai, where the wounded steward was allowed to disembark and the body of the dead woman was taken off to be put into a sealed coffin before being put back on the Jumbo. The airliner sat on the strip in the broiling sun of Dubai for three days, and later one of the passengers, Holger Gauger, a German businessman, said: "We were forced to put our hands on our heads for a total of twelve hours. Anytime there was any action or anyone approached the plane, it was hands up, sometimes for half an hour at a stretch." Yoko Yamamoto, who had been on her way home to Tokyo after a holiday in Europe, said: "We were able to sleep a bit and to eat a little, but it was terrible, horrible."

When the Jumbo eventually took off from Dubai it still did not know where it was going. Saudi Arabia closed its airspace. Kuwait, Abu Dhabi and Bahrein shut their airfields and when the hijackers arrived at Beirut the airport lights were turned off. This forced the hijackers to turn toward Damascus, but they were allowed to land there only because the captain claimed he had engine trouble and three hours later they were in the air again. They headed for their last refuge—Libya. The captain, Kenzi Konuma, said that one of the terrorists remained in his cockpit all the time "armed with a gun and an explosive like a small cake about four inches across." As they drew near to Benghazi airfield in Libya, said Captain Konuma, "they told my passengers they had two minutes after touchdown before the plane would be blown up. I told a hostess to make arrangements for the emergency chutes to be lowered." The passengers began their scramble to safety before the Jumbo had finished rolling. They ran for safety and almost immediately the first charges exploded in the cockpit and the Jumbo burst into flames, providing a spectacular £10 million funeral pyre for the dead terrorist leader. The Arab world was extremely unhappy about this operation. President Qaddafi arrested the Sons of the Occupied Territory and Palestinian leaders in Beirut condemned the hijacking, saying: "This incident, having no nationalistic justification whatsoever and serving none of the goals of the Palestine Revolution, harms the struggle and the prestige of the Palestinians."

The origins and aims of this hijacking are still a mystery. It is not known what happened to the terrorists or even who they were. The Israelis, however, believe that they were certainly PFLP and that one of the Japanese involved was also involved with planning the Red Army massacre at Lod. It may well have been an attempt to demand the freedom of Kozo Okamoto. But it was such a fiasco that nobody wants to claim parenthood.

Less than two weeks later, on August 5, 1973, another group, calling itself "The Seventh Suicide Squad" and claiming that its mission was to exact revenge for the dead Abu Youssef, assassinated by the Israelis in their raid on Beirut, carried out the most vicious and senseless outrage against innocents since the Japanese kamikazes slaughtered the Puerto Rican pilgrims at Lod. Two Palestinians, named as Shafik Hussein el Arida, twenty-two, and Tallal Khaled Kaddourch, twenty-one, pulled out submachine guns and hand grenades at Athens airport, which was crowded with an estimated 1,500 summer tourists, and, with a fusillade of bullets and grenade splinters, reduced the departure lounge to the by now customary shambles of bodies and blood and ruined luggage.

Three people lay dead, two American tourists and an Indian, and fifty-five were wounded. Two of the wounded, one of them a sixteen-year-old American girl, Laura Haack, died in a hospital. Gerald Stern, a dentist from Pittsburgh, described what happened: "The lounge was packed. Many people were buying in the duty-free shop. I saw two Arabs waiting with their suitcases for a security check. An official asked them to open the cases and they took out submachine guns. I threw myself on the floor when the shooting started. All around me people were bleeding and screaming with pain. One of the Arabs was wearing a yellow shirt and the other was in white. Both had their sleeves rolled up. They barricaded themselves behind the bar and fired bursts from their guns. A man next to me had his chest ripped open by bullets. I looked up and saw an old man near the exit trying to run out. He was shot down. I saw someone else with a baby in his arms. He was all covered with blood. Somehow I found an old buddy of mine from school I hadn't seen in ten years. He was shot in the legs."

The terrorists' target was, according to a statement in the Beirut newspaper *Al Nahar,* aimed at passengers on their way to Israel. In fact, most of the victims were waiting to board a TWA flight to New York. When they were formally charged by the Athens public prosecutor, both killers agreed they were members of Black September and said they thought the people they had fired at were American immigrants on their way to Israel and that they were under orders to attack them. The usual statement of justification was addressed to the American people and said: "We have decided to adopt your criminal methods and teach the first lesson to the people who are undertaking a campaign of extermination against us. We have discovered that in order to make you understand us and realize our right to live, we must begin to defend ourselves against all those who seek to exterminate us."

The two killers pleaded guilty when they were put on trial in Athens assize court on January 24, 1974. They said that they had carried out "to the letter" the mission entrusted to them by their Black September leaders. "Our orders were to strike against the passengers of the third TWA aircraft leaving Athens that afternoon, because our leaders had established it was carrying Jewish immigrants to Israel disguised as tourists to settle in the land from which we were uprooted." They admitted that they had bungled their mission and had attacked the wrong group of passengers and said they could not understand how they had made that mistake. "We are very sorry in our hearts that many Greeks were injured," said Arida, "but orders are orders . . . any aircraft of any company that flies to Israel is a target for us." He thus demonstrated once again the fanatical belief of the terrorists that everything is justified and nothing is forbidden to them as long as it serves their cause. Once again this is a harking back to the Assassins, whose motto was: "Nothing is true, and all is permitted."

Arida and Kaddourah were rapidly found guilty of murder of a "particularly odious nature," a crime which carries a mandatory death sentence in Greece. When sentence was pronounced, Arida screamed: "Let's get it over with. Let them kill us. We can't bear solitary confinement anymore." He need not have worried. The Greek government was merely waiting for a chance to pardon them and get rid of them, for they wanted no massacres staged to secure their release. The opportunity came just nine days after the death sentences had been pronounced. A group of terrorists hijacked a Greek ship in Karachi and held the chief officer and chief engineer hostage for thirty-three hours while they demanded the release of Arida and Kaddourah. A deal was worked out. The hostages were released, and after an interval of some weeks during which the Greek court went through the charade of listening to the killers' appeals and going through the judicial procedures, they were pardoned and flown out of the country. It was a very neat operation, and once again terrorists who had carried out a cold-blooded slaughter of innocent people were released to carry on their bloody work.

The next attack came on September 5, the first anniversary of the massacre at Munich. Five Arabs stormed into the Saudi Arabian Embassy in Paris, took thirteen people hostage and issued their ultimatum: Release Abu Daoud or the hostages would be killed. They also demanded a plane to carry them to safety in an Arab country. There followed the usual business of negotiations while terrified noncombatants were threatened with death. The affair lasted twenty-six hours and when it was all over one of the hostages, Mme. Françoise Goussault, the French-born mother of the Earl of Shaftesbury, sat in her Paris apartment drinking champagne, surrounded by telegrams and dozens of red roses and chrysanthemums sent by her friends, and told her story. "Every few hours the gunmen told us that if they did not get a plane they would kill us. We thought they meant what they said." The terrorist leader, she said, was a doctor. "The men with him never referred to his name, it was just 'Doctor.' He was quite good-looking, obviously educated, and I think lived in Jordan. He was polite to me and the French secretary with me. But they were brutal.

"One of the men threatened with shooting jumped out the window. He thought he would be shot in the back, so he told us to give his love to his wife and family. That was one of the brutal episodes; it was the sort of experience I never wish to go through again. Can you picture that scene in the embassy? Hour after hour passing with the doctor getting more angry as the hours passed. And then the threat to kill me and the other French woman if he did not get his way. All we could do was sit and wait. We did get something to eat. A sandwich with something dreadful in it and some tepid water. All we

could do was sit in our chairs and wait for the outcome. We
could hear the noise from the crowd outside—so near and yet
so far away. . . . At one stage they shouted, 'Another ten
minutes and we are going to kill the French ladies.' I was terrified and went to the window and shouted to the Kuwaiti
Ambassador, who was conducting the negotiations, 'Please give
them what they want or they are going to kill us all.' I really
thought they meant it."

Eventually Mme. Goussault, who was secretary to the Saudi
Ambassador, and three other women, were released after the
Iraqi Ambassador volunteered to take their place.

The terrorists took five hostages—their hands bound and
grenades held at their heads—to Le Bourget where they released the Iraqi Ambassador and boarded a Syrian Caravelle.
They flew to Cairo where they turned away PLO representatives
who tried to board the plane, refuelled, then flew on to Damascus where they made a pass at the airfield before flying on to
Kuwait. There another protracted series of negotiations took
place with the terrorists still insisting on their demands for the
release of Abu Daoud. It is interesting to note that they were
calling themselves "the punishment group." And it is possible
that they were concerned not with releasing Abu Daoud but
with getting their hands on him to punish him for spilling the
beans about Black September. At one stage in the negotiations
the "doctor" radioed for an ambulance saying that he had shot
one of the hostages in the leg and would shoot again unless
his demands were met. But he was bluffing and eventually capi-
tulated.

The significance of these autumn incidents is that they
showed a lack of cohesion, an unwillingness by Black September and PFLP to accept responsibility, with the operations
being cloaked in a variety of fancy names and a distinct lack
of enthusiasm by the Arab countries to accept the terrorists.
The Schonau blackmailers flew around the Middle East looking
for sanctuary and were eventually accepted by Libya only as

"an act of humanity." Nobody wanted to accept the Japanese Jumbo. The "Punishment Group" found themselves equally unwelcome wherever they touched down.

Arab disapproval did not stop at the airfields. President Qaddafi arrested the Japanese Jumbo hijackers and Yasir Arafat made a bitter denunciation of the men who attacked the Saudi Embassy in Paris. "It is," he said, "a plot against our people." And he threatened that his organization would seek out and punish whoever was responsible. Arab sources said that the raid was the result of internecine squabbling and was designed to harm Fatah's relations with King Faisal and also to embarrass Arafat while he was attending the conference on nonaligned states in Algiers. It does seem likely that the attack on the Saudi Embassy was a freelance operation, for there was another, much more dangerous operation planned for the anniversary of Munich: the shooting down of an El Al Boeing 707 as it came in to land at Rome airport. Italian police raided a top-floor apartment at Ostia, three miles from Rome's airport, and found there two of Russia's most modern antiaircraft missiles, the SAM 7 Strela (Arrow), hidden in a wardrobe. The rocket launchers, four and a half feet long and weighing thirty pounds, are easily handled by one man and, using an infrared guidance system, are designed to knock down low-flying aircraft up to three miles away. They are so modern that at that time only small numbers had been supplied by the Russians to the Syrian and Egyptian armies.

How, then, did the terrorists come by them? The answer is that they came, unwittingly, from the Egyptian army. It happened during those heady days when it seemed that Colonel Qaddafi was about to fulfill his ambition of uniting Libya and Egypt, and when he heard about the missiles he put pressure on President Sadat to supply some for his army, because, ran his argument, if the two countries are going to be united, then the Libyan army must be trained on the same weapons as the Egyptian soldiers. Sadat was not too keen on this proposition but eventually gave in and gave Qaddafi a small batch "for training purposes only." But Qaddafi had no intention of using them for training. He was still determined to avenge the shooting down of the Libyan airliner in the Sinai by Israeli Phantom fighters. He had tried to get the other Arab countries to take joint action with him against the Israelis when the airliner was shot out of the sky, but had failed. He had no intention, however, of allowing the Israelis to escape without paying in blood for the Libyans they had killed. And so he passed on the SAM 7s to one of the terrorist groups that he financed so that they could exact his revenge. The Italian police claim credit for discovering the SAMs but it is much more likely that they were acting on an Israeli tip-off. The affair had a number of important repercussions. The Egyptians were embarrassed, the Russians were furious and the Americans, to whom the Italians passed on the captured missiles, were delighted to get their hands on one of the latest examples of Russian military gadgetry. It also caused the scare at Heathrow Airport when British troops with orders to "shoot to kill" surrounded the airport with tanks and machine guns, for it was known that the terrorists had more than the two SAMs that were captured at Ostia and it was feared that they had been smuggled into Britain.

The significance of the affair was not lost on Mohammed Hassanein Heikal, a friend of Qaddafi's and, until President Sadat fired him, the most influential newspaperman in the Arab world. Writing in *Al Ahram,* he described the plot to shoot down the airliner as a "scandalous tragicomedy" and argued that had the plotters succeeded, anti-Palestinian sentiments would have been strengthened all around the world. However, Heikal not only influenced, he reflected Arab opinion, and that opinion in the autumn of 1973 had begun to swing away from the support of pure terrorism. It could no longer be claimed that it was necessary to kill in order to bring the Palestinians' plight to the attention of the world. The world now knew all

about the Palestinians, but although the terrorists had succeeded in focusing attention on themselves, they had, for the
main part, excited not sympathy but disgust. The world was
turning against them. Terrorism was becoming counterproductive—despite the refusal of the extremists to learn what was
happening—and the terrorists themselves were in deep trouble.

Despite the desperate autumn rash of incidents they had
still not recovered from the terrible blow inflicted on them by
the Israelis with the raid on Beirut. . . . The CIA had entered
the fight against them after the massacre in Khartoum. . . .
Israeli assassination squads were hunting down their men in
Europe. . . . Moderate Arab opinion was turning against them.
. . . There was dissension within the Palestinian movement.

Black September was in particular trouble. Of all the operations after Beirut, only one was claimed by Black September
and that was the bungled attack at Athens airport. All the
others, apart from Saiqa's "victory" at Schonau, were carried
out either by the PFLP or by the wilder elements of Black
September who had undertaken freelance operations under a
variety of cover names, sometimes in collaboration with Wadi
Haddad's extremists in the PFLP.

There was even a touch of humor for the first time in this
grim story. On August 17, a whisky-drinking Libyan armed
with two pistols hijacked a Boeing 707 of Lebanon's Middle
East Airlines and forced it to fly to Lod. As soon as it landed
—escorted by Phantoms—General Dayan's anti-terrorist squad
went into action and swarmed into the plane to find no terrorist at all, just an old-fashioned drunk full to the brim with
whisky. The plane and its passengers, who included the Libyan
Ambassador to Iraq, flew on to Beirut while the drunk was
carted off to prison. "He will," said Mrs. Meir, "be our guest
for a while."

It was in September that King Hussein dealt the terrorists
the severest blow of all. He flew to Cairo to join President
Assad of Syria and President Sadat to discuss the "reactivation

of the Eastern Front against Israel." Although the world did not know it at the time, it was at this meeting that Sadat and Assad took the final decision to launch the War of the Day of Atonement. But the most immediate result was the welcoming back into the Arab fold of Hussein, the man who had been reviled as a traitor to the Arab cause, who had instigated the slaughter of the commandos in 1970 and who was Number One on Black September's death list. He returned to Amman and celebrated his return to Arab brotherhood by throwing open his prisons and releasing all his political prisoners. There were over a thousand of them. Some were commandos captured in the 1970 fighting, others were political detainees and others were terrorists captured inside Jordan on anti-Hussein missions. The most important among those released were Said al Dajani, a former Jordanian cabinet minister accused of plotting against the King, Saleh Raafat, a leader of Naif Hawatmeh's PDFLP, and Abu Daoud, the man for whose release the Khartoum massacre was staged. Hussein went to the prison, took tea with Abu Daoud and personally supervised his release into the welcoming arms of his family. When last heard of, Abu Daoud was commanding a Fatah detachment facing the Israelis in southern Lebanon during the War of the Day of Atonement.

Hussein's amnesty threw the Palestinian organizations into utter confusion. With one move he gained the support of his archenemy, Assad, and, in Arab eyes, had removed one of the main reasons for Black September's existence. Zuhair Mohsen, leader of the Syrian-backed Saiqa, followed Assad's example and welcomed the Jordanian rapprochement with Egypt and Syria. When the Palestinians' Voice of Syria radio continued to broadcast the same virulent propaganda against Hussein that Assad had previously encouraged, the Syrian leader closed down the station and arrested five of its officials. But Arafat would have none of it. He admitted that the Palestinian movement was facing "embarrassments and restrictions," but blamed it on Hussein and said, "The Hussein of 1973 is the same Hussein of 1970." *Palestine Revolution,* the PLO's news-paper, was deeply critical of the rapprochement, saying that Hussein was "up to his ears in Palestine blood" and had no intention of changing his policy. Arafat called an emergency meeting of the PLO executive in Damascus and there the PLO split straight down the middle, with Zuhair Mohsen supporting the agreement with Hussein while Arafat and the PFLP de-nounced it.

This bitter quarrel among the Palestinians was one more nail in Black September's coffin, and it seemed right that it should be driven in by Hussein, the man whose onslaught on the commandos in September 1970 had given the terrorists both their evocative name and their excuse for killing.

10 • The Day of Atonement

IN THE EARLY afternoon of October 6, 1973, the Day of Atonement, the holiest day in the Jewish calendar, Egyptian troops swarmed across the Suez Canal and Syrian tanks punched an armored fist into the Israeli defenses on the Golan Heights. They came on as no Arab troops had ever done before in the face of the Israelis. The Syrians drove on the very edge of the Golan and looked down on the almost defenseless farmlands of the Galilee. The Egyptians, using the massed firepower of Russian antitank rockets handled by brave, well-trained infantrymen, captured the Bar-Lev line and virtually wiped out the one regular brigade of tanks kept in the Sinai to provide the cover necessary for the mobilization of Israel's civilian army to face any major assault. In the Golan the outnumbered Israelis fought bravely and held on. But in the Sinai they started to crumble under the devastating rocket attacks which incinerated tanks and knocked the Phantoms and Skyhawks of their once invincible air force out of the sky. The Israeli High Command made dreadful errors. There was something akin to panic in the desert headquarters and for two days Israel stood closer to destruction than ever before in its history. But the Egyptians, afraid to emerge from their screen of rockets, did not press their advantage. They gave the Israelis time to mobilize and the Israelis turned with fury on the Syrians, destroying them as an effective fighting force, before switching their attention to the Egyptians, who were now holding a strip of territory some five miles deep on the East Bank of the Canal. It seemed that the Egyptians were there to stay. They planned to whittle away the military and economic strength of Israel in a drawn-out war of attrition. But in one of the most astonishing reversals of fortune in modern warfare, General Arik Sharon led his men back across the Suez in a desperate gamble which, if it had failed, would surely have meant the defeat of Israel. Sharon, however, has gambler's luck—he would have suited Napoleon well—and a ruthless panache and he succeeded to such an extent that his forward troops stopped only an hour's drive from Cairo, the Egyptian Third Army was surrounded, the Second Army was in danger of being rolled up and Egypt was facing a defeat as devastating as that of the Six Day War. It was then that the Super Powers stepped in and ordered a cease-fire, Russia because it could not allow Egypt to be defeated again and the United States because it feared for the future of its detente with Russia and because the oil embargo imposed by the Arab states had begun to bite deeply into the economics of the Western nations—the first effective joint action undertaken by the Arabs in modern times.

And so ended a war which changed everything in the Middle East. The Arabs had regained their lost pride. The Israelis had discovered they were vulnerable. They began to talk peace. The Israelis withdrew from the Canal and, under the tireless urging of Henry Kissinger, it seemed that after all the years of bitterness, enmity and bloodshed a way was being opened for the people of the Arab countries and Israel to live side by side, if not in friendship at least without killing one another.

All this, of course, had a fundamental effect on the Palestinian organizations. While the war was going on they made bombastic claims about military operations undertaken against the Israelis in support of the Syrian and Egyptian armies. Their communiqués made it sound as if they had put a regular army into the field. They claimed to have shot down a Phantom and a Mirage ". . . destroyed several enemy artillery posts . . . caused the destruction of several armored vehicles and the enemy suffered severe loss in its ranks . . . destroyed at several points the railway line between the Sinai and Occupied Palestine in the region of Gaza . . . scored a direct hit on a vehicle carrying Israeli pilots toward Haifa . . . destroyed five of twelve vehicles in a military convoy . . ." Arafat backed these communiqués with an appeal to all Palestinians "inside and outside the occupied territories to direct more strikes against the enemy communication lines, gathering centers and vital installations." But despite this exhortation and the communiqués, the guerrillas' activities amounted to very little; a few rockets lobbed into the northern towns, some mines planted and grenades thrown were all that they could manage. For the first time since 1967 the war against the Israelis was being fought by the regular armies, and the terrorists who had enjoyed the attention of the world for so long were forced to step out of the limelight. At first it did not matter; they were jubilant at the early successes of the Egyptian and Syrian armies and for a time it seemed that their brightest dream was about to be fulfilled—Israel would be destroyed and the Palestinians would regain their lost land. It was not to be, and when Sadat agreed to the cease-fire—an act regarded as a betrayal by the extremists—and actually started to negotiate with the hated enemy, they were thrown into disorder, and the differences between the various organizations became so intense that a danger grew of armed clashes not only between the various organizations but actually inside Fatah between the hard-liners and the moderates. These differences centered on the possibility of Israel being forced by American pressure to disgorge the territory she had swallowed in 1967. The moderates wanted to stake their claim to some of this territory in order to set up a Palestinian state, and to do this they had to go along with Sadat in his peace negotiations. But the hard-liners still rejected this idea of a "mini-state." They still wanted the whole of Palestine returned to Arab rule. It is a quarrel which continues as I write and it is becoming increasingly divisive. On the one hand, there is Arafat and the moderates of Fatah, along with Naif Hawatmeh's Popular Democratic Front for the Liberation of Palestine and the Syrian-backed Saiqa, which will do as President Assad of Syria tells it. On the other is George Habash's PFLP and the wild men of Black September who have abandoned Arafat's Fatah.

Arafat has Sadat's support. The Egyptian President, whose prestige was so greatly enhanced by the October War, accepts Arafat as the "Head of State" of the Palestinians and actually invited Arafat to attend the signing of the Egyptian-Israeli disengagement agreement. Arafat's presence at the signing shocked many of his supporters. The Palestine Liberation Organization, which includes all the commando groups and which has Arafat as its chairman, reacted by issuing a statement saying the agreement "threatened the Palestinian cause with liquidation." But Arafat promptly disowned the statement, claiming that it had been made "illegally." He now seems to have won over the leadership of Fatah to his policies. Even Abu Iyad, the leader of Black September, has fallen into line. It was Abu Iyad who earlier in 1973 told a meeting of the Palestinian Student Union in Cairo that the "strategy of the Palestine Revolution is to wage a long-term struggle and popular war of liberation. . . . We will not accept any solution that would sell our homeland to the usurpers." But now he is playing a key role in preparing

Fatah's rank and file for a radical new approach. "Absolute rejection," he now says, "is sometimes a form of escapism. How long can we go on saying no? Is it not a provisional gain to get back part of our land, 23 percent of Palestine [the West Bank and the Gaza Strip]?" Somehow or other, he says, the guerrillas must insure that on the land evacuated by Israel the Palestinians will set up a "national authority" which can continue the struggle. Naif Hawatmeh agrees. He was the first of the leaders to accept the idea of a Palestinian state on land given up by the Israelis and maintains that such a national authority would indeed be able to "retain its guns and pursue the struggle in all its forms." This is, of course, a far cry from a desire to live in peace with the Israelis. But it is also a far cry from the absolute rejection of any accommodation with them which has always previously been made with such fierceness by men like Abu Iyad. And, while they may continue to call for the overthrow of the State of Israel, there are indications that once the Palestinians are settled on their own piece of territory the urge to continue the bloodshed may subside. There are already signs that the people in whose name the struggle has been waged, the two million refugees, are tired of the never-ending killing. "These are the people who want the Israeli boots out," said one PLO official. "And if they say, 'To hell with you and to hell with King Hussein, we want a Palestinian state,' what are we going to do? Just stand there?" Everything now depends on the Israelis and King Hussein. Will the Israelis give up the territory they seized on the West Bank and will Hussein give up his sovereignty over it to allow the Palestinian state to be set up? The Middle East has had a multitude of prophets and I do not propose to join their number, but certainly both Israel and Hussein will come under enormous pressure from the Super Powers to provide a home for the Palestinian refugees—just as a home was once provided for the Jews.

Another certainty is that the extremists will do their best to wreck any such agreement. George Habash has condemned the Geneva conference as "disgraceful." For him there can be no peace with the Israelis. He and his comrades remain dedicated to the destruction of the State of Israel and to world revolution. With him in opposition to any peace agreement are the young, hard men of Black September who, having been trained and indoctrinated in the use of terror to attack the Israelis, are bewildered by the about-face of Arafat and Abu Iyad. And, once again, there is the strange figure of Colonel Qaddafi. He was outraged when Sadat went to war without consulting him and, while promising financial help to Egypt, sulked in his tent while the war went on. But once Sadat agreed to talk peace, Qaddafi became warlike and threatened to keep the fighting going, "if necessary for a thousand years." The only way he has to do this is to finance terror, and Western intelligence circles are sure that it was Libyan money and ideology which was behind the horrific incident at Rome airport—so often the scene of acts of terror—on December 17, 1973.

Security men going through the baggage of five Arabs found a gun in one of the suitcases. Immediately, all the Arabs pulled out weapons and began shooting. Bullets flew everywhere as the airport police returned the Arabs' fire. The terrorists ran out onto the tarmac, where the Pan American Boeing 707 "Celestial Clipper" was waiting to take off, and threw two phosphorus bombs into the jetliner. It exploded into flames. Passengers and crew threw themselves out of the doors, but many of them had already strapped themselves in and were trapped and burned to death. Thirty-one innocent people died in the inferno of burning fuel and metal, and among them were four Moroccan government officials, fellow Arabs.

As the Boeing burned, the terrorists seized a dozen hostages, boarded a Lufthansa Boeing 707 and forced the captain to take off. They then radioed that they were bound for Beirut, but the Lebanese airport authorities refused to allow them to land and so they ordered the pilot to fly to Athens. They were allowed to land and then, almost as an afterthought, they demanded the relase of Arida and Kaddourah, the Athens airport killers, but these two, who were still awaiting trial, refused to join the hijackers because they said they belonged to a different organization.

It was while these negotiations were going on that the hijackers carried out the cold-blooded killing of one of their hostages, a man who had no possible connection with the Palestinians or their cause. He was Domenico Ippolito, a ground staff worker who had been bundled onto the plane as a hostage. Helen Hanel, an Austrian ground staff employee of Lufthansa who had the misfortune to take cover in the hijacked plane when the shooting started, later described what happened: "They called Mr. Ippolito up from the rear of the plane, where he was sitting alone. He walked up calmly. Nobody had any idea of what was about to happen. They asked him politely, to go into the galley. He walked in and they closed the curtain. Then we heard two shots and it was finished. They threw his body out of the plane. They offered us sandwiches but nobody felt very hungry then."

I know that I will have offended a number of my Arab friends by writing about the fatal flaw of violence in their race. But surely nothing could provide greater evidence of this flaw than the action of this group of killers. Not only did they burn thirty-one people to death, they deliberately took a man's life for no discernible reason. They forced other hostages to scream into the radio while they fired their guns. They told the pilot, Joe Kroese, that they had killed his copilot, Rolf Kiess. And they forced him to say over the radio that he had three dead people on board. They behaved, in fact, with a cruelty which has not been surpassed in any other terrorist operation, and this time, for the first time, a cry of horror arose from the Arab countries as well as the rest of the world. President Sadat denounced their action as "criminal and vicious aggression," and King Hassan of Morocco used similar language, saying that those who died were the "innocent victims of a criminal and vicious aggression which contradicts the noble and human principles and values for which the Arab nation is struggling." Arafat and other guerrilla leaders joined in the condemnation, and when the hijackers finally landed at Kuwait and surrendered, they were arrested and held for questioning by PLO officials.

This Arab reaction stemmed from the belief that the attack, which was carried out just before the Geneva peace conference, was designed to wreck that conference. At first it was thought that the killers were members of one of the extremist groups operating on their own, but then, under questioning in Kuwait, they began to tell an extraordinary story. This story, as it has filtered through to the West, is that they were members of the Arab Nationalist Youth Organization for the Liberation of Palestine, which, although originally formed from a breakaway faction of PFLP, now seems to have developed into a Libyan branch of Black Septembrists who object to Fatah abandoning terrorism in favor of diplomacy.

Their original mission, they said, was not the operation they carried out, but was nothing less than the assassination of Henry Kissinger, the architect of peace in the Middle East. They were to attack his aircraft with their Kalashnikovs and phosphorus bombs when it landed at Beirut. But the Lebanese got wind of the plot and diverted the Secretary of State's plane to the military airfield at Rayak, forty-five miles east of Beirut. It was at about this time that massive security precautions were taken to safeguard Mr. Kissinger wherever his perpetual odyssey took him.

When the plot was thwarted, said the terrorists, they were ordered by their Libyan sponsors to attack Rome airport and to seize hostages with the idea of wrecking the Geneva conference. They were personally sent off by a Libyan diplomat, they said, and their weapons had been sent through the Libyan diplomatic pouch. They also claim that the Libyans offered to insure them for £250,000, payable to their families if they were killed.

It has been suggested in intelligence circles that this story was a "disinformation" plot put out to discredit Qaddafi. In the treacherous byways of Middle East politics anything is possible. Certainly the terrorists' revelations created further shock in the Arab world, and the Libyans, realizing the harm they were doing, called a press conference at which Major Abdul Salam Jalud, the Prime Minister, denied "these fictitious reports. We always support the legitimate struggle of the Palestine people, but our viewpoint on these matters is underlined by our attitude toward hijackers who have landed in Libya. The Palestinian resistance movement must act within Palestine." This position is quite at variance with Qaddafi's earlier attitude toward terrorism and it is generally believed that Jalud was put up to provide a smokescreen for the Libyan involvement in an operation that got out of hand. However, in February 1974, Qaddafi began to make conciliatory gestures toward President Sadat and it is possible that he too might have been shocked by the results of his plotting, and realizing the strength of Sadat's position as "the commando of peace," decided to cut his losses and go along with the peace settlement.

If so, with Arafat and Sadat so eager for peace, and with the possibility of the Israelis giving up enough land to form a Palestinian state, it may well be that Black September's short but bloody story has ended. Its last admitted operation was at Athens in August 1973. There was nothing between then and the time of writing, May 1974, and that is a long time in terrorist terms.

But the death of Black September does not mean that Arab terrorism will end. There are still those who hope to wreck the peace. There are the dissident Black Septembrists who refuse to accept Fatah's new policy and still dream of destroying Israel. And there is still George Habash with his dreams of world revolution. Terrorism is the only weapon they have. Black September may die. The PFLP may die in its turn. But new secret societies will spring up to take their place in the cruel tradition of the Assassins, for the fatal flaw still exists and will not be eradicated until many years have passed in which the Arabs have enjoyed peace, prosperity and pride. At a meeting in Cairo to eulogize the Palestinian leaders killed by the Israelis in the raid on Beirut, I listened to an impassioned speech by one of their comrades in which he said: "Death is the door to a happy future for our people." There spoke the voice of the Assassins.

Index

Abdullah, King of Jordan, 3, 5, 19
Aboussan, Ahmed, 104
Adwan, Kamal, 121, 122, 123
Adwan, Maha, 121–22
Afghani, Ahmed, 46
Ahlers (Bonn spokesman), 86
Alon, Col. Yosef, 105, 106
Amer, Gen. Hussein Sirry, 4
Amin, President of Uganda, 113
Amir, Rehavam, 107, 108
Anderson, Miriam, 67
Arab-Israeli wars, 23
    June War, 17, 23, 24
    1947–1948, 14
    October War, 162–66
    Suez Affair, 15
    See also June War; October War;
      Suez Affair
Arab Legion, 14
Arab Liberation Front, 26, 52
Arab Nationalist Youth Organiza-

tion for the Liberation of Pal-
    estine, 100, 101, 102, 169
Arabs
    history, 4–8, 19–23, 56, 57–61
    oil embargo, 163
    support for Palestinian resistance,
      8–9, 51–52, 53, 55, 57, 158–59
    See also Palestinians; names of
      Arab nations
Arafat, Yasir
    and Black September, 42, 50–51,
      148
    and Brotherhood, 6
    criticism of resistance operations,
      30, 81, 119, 157, 165, 167, 169
    Fatah leadership role, 16, 18, 38,
      121, 122, 131, 132, 145
    and Hussein, 34, 160–61
    and Israeli Beirut raid, 124–25
    political philosophy, 62
    and Sadat, 165

Arguello, Patrick, 32, 72
Arida, Shafik Hussein el, 152, 154, 168
Assad, President of Syria, 159, 160, 165
Assassins, Society of, 6–7, 12, 154
Assifa, el, 16
Athens, airport operation (Aug. 5, 1973), 57, 152–55, 168
Atrash, Abdel Aziz el, 67
Auda, Abdul el Kader, 5
Aurore, L' (Paris), 104, 105
Austria, Black September organization in, 139–43
Avimor, Simon, 107
Awad, Ahmed Mousa, 67

Baader-Meinhof group, 69, 70, 114, 134
Baghdady, Jawal Khalil, 2
Balfour Declaration (Nov. 2, 1917), 21–22
Bangkok, Israeli Embassy operations
(Dec. 28, 1972), 97, 107–109
(March 1973), 46, 116, 121
Banna, Hassan el, 4, 6, 11
Barakat, Daoud, 135, 148
Bardali, Nadia and Marlene, 138–39
Barges, Evelyn, 104
Bar-Lev, Lt. Gen. Haim, 34
Bar-Lev, Capt. Uri, 32–33, 145
Bashir, Hussein, 99–100
Ben Gurion, David, 22
Berger, David, 87
Bernadotte, Count Folke, 90
Black September
Arab support for, 51–52
Bangkok operation, 107–109
Cairo Sheraton operation, 1–4, 10–11, 12, 40
development, 39–41
European organization and operations, 134–49
goals, 62–64
Jordanian Ambassador operation, 12–14
Khartoum operation, 112–19
leadership and organization, 6,
43–44, 45–46, 77–78, 135, 150
Lod airport operation, 66–69
Munich operation, 80–88
name origin, 3, 34
and other Palestinian resistance groups, 42–43, 47, 50, 70, 132, 150–61
and Revenging Palestinians, 37, 38–39
BOAC, hijacking (Sept. 9, 1970), 33
Bouchki, Ahmed, 106
Boudia, Mohammed, 104–105, 138
Boumedienne, Houari, 104
Brandt, Willy, 83
Brotherhood, Moslem, 4–5, 12, 59
Burg, Yosef, 88

Cairo, Sheraton Hotel operation
(Nov. 28, 1971), 1–4, 10–11, 12, 40
Campbell-Lefevre, Diane, 97–98, 144
CENTO, 126
Central Intelligence Agency (CIA), 117, 126, 127, 159
Cohen, Baruch, 103
Comay, Michael, 92
Cyprus, 100–102

Dajani, Said el, 160
Daoud, Abu, 40, 46, 47, 114, 117, 155, 156, 160
Munich operation role, 81
captured, 47–49
Dayan, Gen. Moshe, 66, 69, 106, 159
De Gaulle, Charles, 23, 137

Eagles of the Palestinian Revolution, 140, 142
Eaks, Louis, 144
East Germany, 133
Eban, Abba, 108
Egypt
Munich operation role, 83
October War role, 162, 163, 164
Eid Guy, 49, 114, 115
EL AL
hijackings, 29, 31–32, 78

office attacks, 30
shooting, 33
Elath, sinking, 25
Elazar, Gen. David, 66, 67, 123
Essawy, Mustapha el, 108, 109
Esso Oil, 65
Etherington-Smith, Raymond, 113, 114
Evelyne, 138, 139
Eyal, Yigal, 106

Faisal, King, 59, 113, 157
Fallaci, Oriana, 31
Farghaly, Sheikh Mohammed, 5
Farouk, King, 4, 15
Farrau, Rex, 91
Farrau, Roy, 91
Fatah, Al
  Arab support for, 16–17, 23, 39
  and Black September, 39–43, 49–50, 117–18, 148
  "Black September" massacre, 33–41
  founding, 15–16, 46, 132
  in Germany, 132–33
  goals, 62–64
  Israeli Beirut raid on, 124
  and Khartoum operation, 115, 116
  operations, 17, 24, 65
  organization and leadership, 6, 48, 121, 131, 132, 165
Federal Bureau of Investigation (FBI), 126
Figaro, Le (Paris), 33
Flame of Islam, The (Lamb), 7
France, Black September organization in, 137–39
Frangie, Suleiman, 131
Franji, Abdullah al, 131–32
Frisch, Lt. Col. Abraham, 75
Fuheid, Mohammed Abdul Karin, 145–46
Fukunaga, Kinji, 72

Gassan, Rizig Abu, 118
Gauger, Holger, 151
General Union of Palestinian Students, 132–33

General Union of Palestinian Workers, 132–33
Geneva peace negotiations (1973–74), 169
George, Lloyd, 21
Germany
  Munich operation role, 83–86
  Palestinian resistance organization and operations in, 33, 131–33, 134–35
Gilzer, Simha, 100, 119
Gladnikoff, Marianne, 107
Goodhart, Philip, 149
Goussault, Françoise, 155–56
Great Britain, Black September organization in, 143–49
Grigg, Lee, 61–62
Gulf Oil, 65, 138

Habash, George, 26, 30, 31, 33, 53, 61–62, 69, 72, 89, 128, 144, 165, 167, 170
Hacker, Friedrich, 142
Hadaf, Al, 76
Hadas, Nitzan, 109
Hadas, Ruth, 109
Hadassah Hospital (Mount Scopus), 90
Haddad, Wadi, 30, 33, 70, 76, 89, 159
Hakim, Jamil Abdel, 97
Halsa, Therese, 67, 68, 69, 72, 108
Hammani, Said, 148
Hamshari, Mahmoud, 99, 104
Hanel, Helen, 168
Haroun al Rashid, 19
Hasham, Adnam Ali, 78
Hassan, Hani al, 132
Hassan, King of Morocco, 168
Hassan ibn Sabah, 6, 7, 8
Hassouna, Khalek, 3
Hatim, Abu, 50
Hawatmeh, Naif, 26, 76, 122, 130, 165, 166
Heikal, Mohammed Hassanein, 158
Helou, Ziad, 2, 11, 121
Hodeiby, Hassan el, 5
Hussein, King of Jordan, 3, 10, 12, 13, 18, 30, 33, 49, 54, 129, 159, 160–61, 166

Husseini, el (Mufti of Jerusalem),
6, 12
Abdel Kader, 6, 46
Haj Amin, 5–6, 12, 18
Zaid, 6

Ippolito, Domenico, 168
IRA, 46, 69, 96, 144
Irgun Zvai Leumi, 90, 100
Israel
airport security systems, 96
anti-Arab history, 90
anti-Palestinian campaigns, 98–
100, 104–105, 119–25, 127
Beirut raid by (Apr. 10, 1973),
30, 40, 43, 46, 119–25, 127
car bomb security, 97
embassy security, 94–97
intelligence operations, 128–29
Karameh attack, 24–25
Lebanon raids, 129–30
letter bombs sent by, 91, 93
October War role, 162, 163, 164,
166
"007" squad, 32
PFLP attacks by, 89–90
shooting down Libyan Boeing
(Feb. 21, 1973), 110–12, 158
Italy, Black September organization
in, 136–37, 158
Iyad, Abu, 43–44, 45, 48, 50, 70,
81, 121, 122, 148, 165, 166,
167
Iyad, Abu Ali, 37, 39, 40

JAL, hijacking (July 20, 1973), 47,
150–52
Jalud, Maj. Abdul Salam, 170
Jerusalem, 5, 60–61
Jibril, Ahmed, 76
Jordan, 11, 33–37, 114
June War (1967), 17, 23, 24, 36

Kaddourch, Tallal Khaled, 152,
154, 168
Kalthoum, Oum, 59
Kanafani, Ghassan, 89, 90
Kannon, Khodr, 103
Karam (Fatah member), 118
Karameh, Battle of, 24–25

Katchalsky, Aharon, 71
Kedouri, Eli, 12
Kennedy, Joseph P. III, 52
Kennedy, Robert F., 114
Kershaw, Anthony, 114
Khaldo, Mahmoud, 140
Khaled, Leila, 32, 33, 72, 145
Khalifa, Monzer, 2, 11, 121
Khalil, Abu, 93
Khalil, Sakar Mahmoud al, 97
Khartoum, Saudi Embassy opera-
tion (March 1, 1973), 49, 50,
54, 57, 112–19, 125
Khelfa, Frazeh, 13
Kiess, Rolf, 168
King David Hotel, 90
Kissinger, Henry, 163, 169
KLM, hijacking, 102
Konuma, Capt. Kenzi, 152
Kreisky, Bruno, 8, 141–42
Kroese, Joe, 168
Kronawitter (Munich mayor), 86
Kubeisy, Dr. Bassel Rauf, 103–104,
119

Laird, Melvin, 93
Lamb, Harold, 7
Latif, Mahmoud Abdul, 5
Lawrence of Arabia, 21
Lebanon, 129, 130–31
Leber, Georg, 52
Levy, Reginald, 66, 67
Liberation Front (Iran), 70
Libya, 111
Lod, airport operations
Red Army (Japanese) (May 30,
1972), 53, 54, 57, 70–75, 87,
89, 90, 98, 111, 112, 152
Sabena hijacking (May 8, 1972),
66–69
Lufthansa, hijackings, 8, 52–53, 86

Macomber, William, 115
Mahler, Horst, 134
Maitland, Donald, 128
Makarios, President of Cyprus, 102
Marks and Spencer (London),
bombing, 146
Marron, Hannah, 31
Masalhah, Mohammed, 82, 83, 84

Meir, Golda, 86, 88, 90, 93–94, 98, 106, 123, 141, 159
Merck, Dr. Bruno, 85
Meyer, Armin, 125–26
Moharrer, Al, 105, 142
Mohsen, Zuhair, 160, 161
Mongols, Middle East invasion, 12, 20
Moore, George, 49, 113, 114, 115, 117
Moslem Brotherhood. *See* Brotherhood
Mufti of Jerusalem, 14, 51. *See also* Husseini, el
Munich, Olympic Games operation, 46, 47, 49, 50, 52, 54, 80–88, 112, 131–32, 134, 135, 144

Nahar, Al, (Beirut), 153
Nakaa, Abdel Hadi, 137
Napoleon, 20
Nashashibi, Nasir ad-Din an-, 9–10
Nasser, Gamal Abdel, 4, 5, 15, 16, 17, 25, 29, 34, 38, 86
Nasser, Kamal, 121, 122, 123
Nathan, Asher Ben, 149
NATO, 126
Nazzal, Yusuf, 81, 82, 83
Neguib, General, 5
Nimeiry, President of Sudan, 50, 113, 117, 118
Nixon, Richard M., 93, 115, 117, 125
Noel, Cleo, 49, 113, 114, 115

Obote, Milton, 113
October War (1973), 60, 160, 162–66
Okamoto, Kozo, 71, 72, 73–75, 76, 108, 151, 152
Okidoro, Takeshi, 71
Olivares, Vittorio, 104
Olympic Games operation. *See* Munich
Organization of Victims of Zionist Occupation, 52

Palestine Liberation Army, 16
Palestine Liberation Organization (PLO), 40, 145, 165

Arab support for, 51
founding, 16
leadership, 10, 18, 122, 161
Rome airport operation role, 169
Palestinian Revolution, The (Fatah monthly), 62, 161
Palestinians, resistance movement
goals, 62–64
history, 14–17, 56
in Jordan, 18–19
Jordan River ambushes, 26–29
letter bombs sent by, 91–93
October War role, 164, 165–67
organizations, 26
See also names of specific groups
Pan American Airlines, hijacking, 31–32
Paris, Saudi Embassy operation, 155–56
Parsons, William, 12
Pasha, Nokrashy, 11
People's Liberation Army (Turkey), 70
Peres, Shimon, 92
Philosophy of the Revolution (Nasser), 4
Pilz, Dr. Adolf, 91
Popular Democratic Front for the Liberation of Palestine (PDFLP), 26, 76, 165
Israeli raid on headquarters, 122–23
leadership, 160
Popular Front for the Liberation of Palestine (PFLP)
and Black September, 42, 70, 78
Cyprus operations, 100–102
financing, 52, 53
goals, 26, 39, 77
international resistance meeting, 69–70
leadership, 26, 89, 103–104, 165
Lod airport operation, 70–75, 89, 90
operations, 29–30, 31–34, 39, 62, 147
origins, 75
philosophy, 31
Red Army alliance, 72, 73, 74, 75

Index

Popular Front for the Liberation of Palestine—General Command, 76, 79
Praphas, Charasathien, 108
Prins, Vivian, 92
Provenza, Dr. Bonaventura, 137
Punishment Group, 49, 156

Qaddafi, Colonel
  and JAL hijacking, 152, 157
  and Khartoum operation, 112, 113, 116, 118, 119
  and Libyan Boeing shooting, 111
  and Sadat, 157–58, 167, 170
  support for Palestinian resistance, 10, 11, 52, 53
Quamiyin al Arab, 75–76

Raafat, Saleh, 160
Rabah, Essat, 2, 3, 11, 121
Razd (Fatah intelligence), 45, 98, 104, 136
Red Army group (Japanese), 53, 70–75, 152
Red Cross, 66
Redding, Jean, 103
Republique, La (Algeria), 125
Return Ticket (Nashashibi), 9–10
Revenging Palestinians, 37, 65
Rifai, Zaid el, 12–13, 45, 146, 149
Rogers, William P., 29, 93
Romano, Joseph, 83
Rome, airport operation (Dec. 17, 1973), 167
Rothschild, Lord, 21

Sabena, hijacking, 46, 66, 116, 121
Sadat, Anwar el, 83
  and Bangkok operation, 108
  and Brotherhood, 4
  and Khartoum operation, 115–16
  Libyan alliance, 157–58
  October War role, 159–60, 164, 165
  political role, 170
  and Rome airport operation, 168
Said, Nuri, 59
Saiqa, El (Syria), 26, 52, 140, 142, 160, 165
Saladin, 20, 57, 58

Salameh, Ali Hassan, 6, 45, 47, 107
Salameh, Sheik Hassan, 45
Saleh, Zaharia Abu, 104
Sanya (Cypriot ship), 119
Saudi Arabia, 8
Schonau Castle, operation, 8, 140, 141–43
Schreiber, Manfred, 85
Scotland Yard, 13
Secret Organ, 4
Sekigun, Rengo, 53
Selassie, Emperor Haile, 113, 118
Seventh Suicide Squad, 152–55
Shachori, Dr. Ami, 91, 92, 146
Sharon, Gen. Arik, 163
Shemali, Fuad, 46, 70, 135
Sherif, Bassam Abu, 76, 77, 89, 126
Shibli, Hamit Abdul, 137
Shiga, Dr. Willibald, 142
Shin Bet (Israeli intelligence), 32, 86
Shukairy, Ahmed, 10, 16, 17
Sidki, Azziz, 53, 83
Sieff, Joseph "Teddy", 146–47
Sirhan, Sirhan, 114, 117
Six Day War. See June War
Society of Assassins. See Assassins
Sons of the Occupied Territory, 151–52
Soudeidan, Mustafa, 140
Soviet Union, 158
  June War role, 36
  October War role, 163, 166
Stern, Gerald, 153
Stern Gang, 90, 91
Streuber Motor Company (Germany), 65
Sudan, 114, 115
Suez Affair (1956), 15, 23, 24, 25
Sunchai Pienkama, 107
Sunday Telegraph (London), 142
Swissair, hijackings, 30, 31–32
Switzerland, Black September organization in, 33, 135–36
Syria
  "Black September" massacre role, 35, 36
  Fatah support, 17
  October War role, 162, 163, 164

Tabab, Mohammed, 97
Tamerlane, 20
Tannous, Rima, 67, 68, 69, 72, 108
Tekoah, Josef, 92
Tell, Wasfi, 1, 2-3, 10, 13, 37, 39, 40, 46, 116, 121
Tell, Mrs. Wasfi, 2, 3
Teloria, Manuel, 146
Thanon Kittikachorn, 108
Thawra, Al (Syria), 125
Timor, Rahamin, 95, 100
Trieste, trans-Alpine oil terminal, 78, 104
TWA, hijacking, 31-32

Ulbricht, Walter, 86
Umari, Fakhri al, 47, 81, 82, 83
United Nations, 128
United States
    and Beirut raid, 124-25
    Khartoum demands on, 114-15
    and Middle East, 125-26
    October War role, 163, 165, 166
    Sixth Fleet threat, 35

Vider, Shlomo, 32
Vijiralongkorn, Crown Prince, 107
Voice of Palestine, 55, 87, 105, 125

War of Attrition. *See* Suez Affair
War of the Day of Atonement. *See* October War
Wazir, Khalil al, 46, 70, 132
Weinberg, Moshe, 83
World War I, 20, 21

Yamamoto, Yoko, 151
Yariv, Maj. Gen. Aharon, 90, 98
Yashuda, Yasuiki, 71, 72
Yassin, Deir, 90, 91
Yassin, Fawaz, 118
Yemen (People's Democratic Republic of South Yemen), 53
Young Liberals (Great Britain), 114
Youssef, Abu, 40, 46, 116, 121, 122, 123, 152

Zadok, Ophir, 102-103
Zaid, Ahmed, 78
Zeevi, Gen. Rehaven, 68, 72
Zeid, Mustafa Awadh Abu, 93
Zeiton, Hannan Claude, 71
ZIM lines, 146
Zionists/Zionism, 21
Zoller, Capt. Erwin, 52
Zwaiter, Wael, 98